THE QUANTUM HUMAN

*Understanding the Evolution of
Consciousness, the Solar Plexus Mutation,
and Human Design*

KAREN CURRY PARKER

For permissions contact:

An Imprint for GracePoint Publishing (www.GracePointPublishing.com)

322 N Tejon St. #207
Colorado Springs CO 80903
www.GracePointMatrix.com
Email: Admin@GracePointMatrix.com
SAN # 991-6032

ISBN-13: (Paperback) #978-1-951694-25-8
eISBN: (eBook) # 978-1-951694-26-5

Books may be purchased for educational, business, or sales promotional use.
For bulk order requests and price schedule contact:
Orders@GracePointPublishing.com

Printed in the United States of America

To run your chart with the new Quantum Human design language go to www.FreeHumanDesignChart.com & to find out more about the Quantum Alignment System (TM) visit https://www.quantumalignmentsystem.com/

Included in this book is a free course on the Solar Plexus mutation. At the end of each chapter, you will find a QR code that you can scan with your phone or click and it will take you directly to the chapter lesson. We hope you enjoy this upgraded book service.

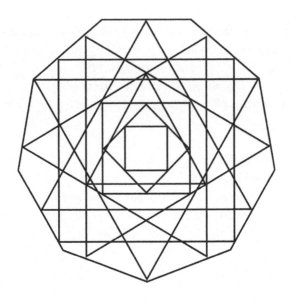

TABLE OF CONTENTS

A Note for You vii

Dedication ix

Introduction xi

Chapter 1 - Global Cycles and the Solar Plexus Mutation.... 1

Chapter 2 - The Mechanics of Creating.................................21

Chapter 3 - The Evolving Heart.......................................41

Chapter 4 - Situational Creativity versus
　　　　　　Fundamental Creativity 77

Chapter 5 - From the Cross of Planning to the
　　　　　　Cross of the Sleeping Phoenix: A Test
　　　　　　of Time, Faith, and Alignment...................... 107

Chapter 6 - The Mechanics of the Shift 129

Chapter 7 - Putting It All Together 145

References.. 159

About the Author 165

A Note for You

This book is for all of you who know what you know but don't always know how you know.

It is for those of you who have struggled to find the words to explain to others who doubt what you know as truth in your heart.

This information is for those of you who were told that your "knowing" wasn't enough.

It is for those of you who listened to the words of others and doubted yourself instead of questioning their need to make you prove your own knowingness.

This book is for those of you who, over the course of your life and your education, mistakenly bought into the belief that you are not enough, not brilliant, not creative, not powerful, not successful, not lovable, not worthy, not wise, or any other story you were told that caused you to believe that you are less than the breathtakingly awesome once-in-a-lifetime cosmic event that you are.

This book is for you because when you reclaim the truth of who you are, you not only create a life that is worthy of you, you also take your place in service to the world, by being who you truly are.

Dedication

Being on the leading edge isn't always comfortable.

Every day I coach people who never really felt like they "fit in". I like to call these people "Starseeds."

These "Starseeds", who as children, stood out under the night sky and wondered when they could go "home", who knew they were here on a "mission", and who fought the heaviness of the karmic burden of this planet, have always known what was ahead for us on Earth.

I have had the privilege of listening to the voices of Starseeds for most of my life. They have endured bullying, abuse, ridicule, and the pain of feeling the gap between reality and the human potential. These sensitive souls have served as stewards for the coming era of Peace under the most challenging of circumstances.

They have held the template of a New Earth in their Hearts and sought to build it with their hands. They have been quietly serving in the trenches as Lightworkers, healers, farmers, innovators, and teachers.

This book is for the Starseeds. I hope it gives you hope that we're almost done and that your lives have been an essential part of building the foundation of a world of sustainable, just, and equitable peace for all.

May your voices gain strength. May your vision stay clear and strong. May your wisdom lead us on the path forward.

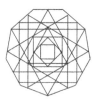

Introduction

Our true nature is to be creative. We are all, each and every one of us, powerful creative beings who use our perceptions to create our collective and individual experience of reality. Our collective consciousness is evolving. Evolution in consciousness is not only showing up as new scientific understandings about how the world works, it is literally manifesting as physical changes in the way in which our brains and bodies work.

The rate at which we are evolving is reaching a pace at which the old systems we created with Material Consciousness are no longer working for the majority of people. Our current education systems perpetuate an outdated way of thinking that causes children to feel that they are broken, stupid, disruptive, non-creative or in any way "less than".

Our health care system treats people based on their material value and with limited models that do not take into account non-locality and fully integrative aspects of wellness and perception as part of the healing process.

Our economy is driven by materialism, inequality, and excludes people from participating fully. In an evolving world where the concept of value is changing dramatically, the old economy is no longer sustainable.

Even the way in which we organize our communities and our government is in need of a serious overhaul as we begin to realize that affecting real, sustainable, peaceful change on the planet will require us to first and foremost change our perceptions about what we believe is possible to experience on Planet Earth.

We would not be realistic if we didn't take stock of our current perceptions of the world and examine what these perceptions are creating. We live in a world where there is mounting scientific evidence that we are facing a global crisis—a crisis rooted in a consciousness and perception of lack.

We are deeply conditioned by old material consciousness, which is based on a model of finite resources, zero-sum game thinking and, by nature, competition. We are afraid that we lack the resources, food, water, money, systems of allocation and management, education, opportunity or knowledge to make the changes necessary to surmount the global challenges facing us today.

Our collective perceptions of lack are created from our own individual stories of personal lack. Each and every one of us who is in some way living the story of "not enough" and creating the manifestation—the collapse —of the quantum potential of lack and is adding to the experience of lack on the planet.

The perception of lack creates less than enough, accompanied by naysaying, doubt, and the denial of "unrealistic" possibilities. When we think we are not enough, don't have enough, aren't worthy of more, and play in a limited, zero-sum game, then that is what we inevitably create in the world. When we come from a place of lack, the dreamers who bring us the fantastical ideas, such as going to the moon, are shut down, laughed at, and denied the opportunity to assist with the evolution of humanity.

The dreamers, the creatives, the leaders on the edge of consciousness know—sometimes without knowing exactly how they know (but they do!)—that they have the answers to saving the world, the answers to creating a world of sustainable peace and sustainable resources. When we shut down the dreamers, we shut down the possibility of what else is possible for the planet.

Right now, on this planet, there are people who carry the seeds of inspiration, the root ideas for creating the next phase of humanity on the planet. In our midst are people who have the next new idea that can change the definition of what's possible for humanity, much like space travel changed our idea of who we are and what we can achieve.

For us to be ready to serve as sacred stewards for these ideas, to plant them, tend to them and, ultimately, collapse the quantum potentials that will make them manifest in the world, we have to remember our natural creative power and unlock the full potential of our human creative genius.

In this book you're going to learn about the mechanics of the evolution of humanity through the lens of Quantum Human Design, a system that teaches you how to fulfill your life and soul purpose using a blend of several ancient esoteric systems including the Chinese I'Ching, the Hindu Chakra system, Judaic Kabbalah, and astrology.

The information shared in this book is based on the basic information first revealed by Ra Uru Hu, the founder of traditional Human Design. It offers, however, an alternative perspective on the evolution of the world and shares a message of hope and empowerment.

As a student of Ra, I am grateful for Ra and his understanding of the mechanics of the shift on the planet. His work and his life are a testament to his courage and his willingness to transmit a body of information that has the potential to transform the way we love and nurture each other in a rapidly changing world.

Your Quantum Human Design is calculated using your birthday, time and place and, just like with astrology, the system is based on a chart that is generated by computer. (If you need to calculate your chart or the chart of your loved ones, please visit www.freehumandesignchart.com).

You are NOT your Quantum Human Design chart.

Your chart is not the definition of Who You Are.

Your chart is simply a map of your "soul curriculum", what you came here to experience, do and be on this planet at this vital time.

YOU are an infinite, powerful creator, living in a human story.

All the other details of your story - your religion, your race, your gender, your enneagram, your astrology chart, your numerological profile, your political party affiliation, your nationality, your job title, define aspects of your story, but they do not tell the full story of who you truly are.

I'll say it again because it's so important. YOU are an infinite, powerful creator, living in a human story.

I'm going to add one more thing.

Before I started writing this book, I set the intention for this note to reach all of us who may have gotten swept up and confused by the centuries of hidden pain that we are all healing on the planet right now and see this nugget of a reminder.

Here's what I gently remind you:

If you're reading this book, your soul was called to this planet to do one thing and that "thing" is the most important thing you can do - fulfill your life purpose.

Your life purpose isn't your work or what you do. Your life purpose is to be the fulfilled expression of who you came here to be in this lifetime. You ARE your life purpose.

For a lot of us, when we read those words, it might inspire a certain amount of panic. Many of us "know" that we are here for a reason, but we might not remember what that reason is.

You came here to heal centuries of hidden pain so that the echoes of this pain can be permanently wiped off the planet.

You came here to free yourself from the bondage of a consciousness of lack so that you could turn around and do the same for others.

**So we can learn to create from a place of infinite power.

**So we can live from abundance, not scarcity.

**So we can create a world of equitable, sustainable peace.

**Because a world of equitable, sustainable peace is the fulfillment of the human potential.

That's your mission.

For some of you that might mean spending a lifetime of clearing trauma from your cells and the cells of others.

For others, it might mean to stop making excuses - albeit clever ones - that are keeping you from fulfilling your purpose. It is TIME for you to share your message, write that book, create that program, do your life's work and stop hiding out.

You are absolutely worthy of serving the divine mission of transforming, aligning and healing this world by being who you are.

This book is designed to be a guide for you to activate your own remembering of the mission of evolution and the natural creative power that you were born with. When you fully embody your natural creative power and you clear the generations of conditioning and ancestral pain your cells are carrying, you will be fulfilling your ultimate purpose, to use your creative power to create an equitable, sustainable world of peace.

To do that you have to do one crucial thing:

Bring yourself back into alignment with living true to who you really are.

You are a once-in-a-lifetime cosmic event. You are an intentional soul living a temporary life story with a purpose. Over the course of your life you've experienced joys, traumas, pain and love; you've been conditioned by the mindsets, beliefs, and energies from the people who have played a major part in your life.

You are also carrying within your cells the energy of ancestral memories that are stored in your DNA. The emerging science of epigenetics has shown us that many of our reactions, anxieties, fears, and even our tendency to express certain gene regulators are actually influenced by events that happened in our family lineage up to fourteen generations before we were born.

In other words, things that happened in your ancestral lineage are influencing the DNA your family is carrying. This genetic influence is inherited, and we all carry genetic memory of things that happened on the planet before we incarnated.

Your life experiences and your genetic programming (and more) can often entrain or condition you away from being the person you were born to be. Your conditioning influences your perception and consequently which quantum potentials you make manifest in your life.

To activate your mission on the planet at this time, you have to de-condition yourself. You have to create a new set of meanings and perspectives that are empowering. You have to re-program your DNA.

You have to fully activate the power of your soul expressing its true creative capacity so that your human story can fulfill its full purpose—to heal the world.

When you do this, your capacity to intentionally harness your natural creative power increases exponentially.

CHAPTER 1

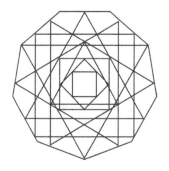

Global Cycles and the Solar Plexus Mutation

The word "imagine" is one of the most powerful words in the English language.

Before we could even build a rocket ship, an imaginative soul stood outside under the shining light of the night sky and dreamt that one day humans would travel beyond the blue and into space to visit the moon.

I don't know how the rest of this person's story unfolds, but it's easy to imagine them sitting at a table enjoying a glass of wine with friends and, when they felt courageous enough, leaning forward and sharing with passion their vision of people traveling to the moon.

I can hear the laughter in response, see the looks of disbelief on their friend's faces, and imagine them crediting the good wine as the source of their friend's "inspiration".

And yet, in spite of ridicule, disbelief, and maybe even generations of time, the vision initiated by this dreamer became a reality on July 20, 1969, when the first human walked on the moon, forever changing what we think is possible.

Since the Age of Enlightenment and the Scientific Revolution, humanity has been on a quest to understand the nature of our reality. Logic, reasoning, and scientific philosophies have crafted our cultural perspectives forcing us into formulaic ways of thinking and understanding the world. Science has given us answers that help us make sense of our lives and the material world around us.

We have physical laws and formulas that explain the movement of matter, biological theories and formulas that explain evolution, and chemical theorems and formulas that explain how materials interact with each other. We've even used our scientific formulas to try to prove (or disprove) the existence of God.

Logic, the currency of science, teaches us to look for formulas and to use patterns to predict future outcomes. We've used logic to not only predict the efficacy of pharmaceuticals and therapies and to "prove" our theories about how the world works, but also to create models that paint a bleak future for humanity, a future where global warming decreases our capacity to feed, shelter and protect the large number of people on the planet.

The human brain has two hemispheres, each responsible for two distinctly different ways of processing information. The left hemisphere tends to be more responsible for logical and linear thinking. We tend to think of this traditionally as "masculine" thinking. The right hemisphere is more associated with emotional, sensing and holistic "big picture" ways of thinking. Right brain functions tend to be more associated with art and creativity and "feminine" ways of thinking.

Most people tend to use one side of the brain more than the other. Because the brain is so malleable, our conditioning and our education can cause us to develop one side of the brain more than the other. Most of us are deeply conditioned by our education and the world around us to draw more strongly and consistently from the left (logical) side of the brain.

We are so in love with science and logic that we judge all other ways of human knowing as "unreasonable". We consider "logic" to be the only "reasonable" way to know if anything is true or not, discounting intuition, sensing and experiential wisdom.

We've applied the notion of logical reasoning and systems to every aspect of our human lives. We have a factory model system in the workplace. Our school system is based on science and educational research. Our healthcare system is scientifically driven. We even have scientific models to help us predict the outcome of political elections.

Formulaic thinking requires us to distill concepts and ideas into particles or categories. If you are going to follow a formula, you have to know the parts in order to know what constitutes the outcome of the whole: A + B = C.

The education system, the institution that is responsible for training us "how" to think, has broken the formula of teaching young humans into parts called subjects. As early as kindergarten, the curriculum is chunked down into the pieces of the education formula: science, math, reading, writing, and, rarely, art, music, and movement of some kind.

Creativity can sometimes seem like serendipity or an adjunct, non-vital way of experiencing the world. We relegate creativity as something we do on the side, as a hobby or a way to unwind and relax. Creativity and the subjects that enhance creativity are considered "extras" and not vital parts of the educational formula.

When we eliminate creativity from our collective systems, such as the education system, and we only support a logical, linear system that teaches us that creativity is "extra", we not only lock out the possibility of success for two thirds of our population, we also limit our ability to tap into the powerful creative solutions to the challenges facing humanity today. We are facing a crisis and if we only look to linear, scientific formulas for the answers, we run the risk of missing the possibility of genuine change available to us.

Neuroscientists and quantum physicists are beginning to understand that there is actually science behind creativity and that, when we understand the science of creativity, we can consciously harness our creative power and find elegant solutions to the challenges facing humanity. Creativity allows us to be more resilient during times of rapid change and increases our ability to withstand stress and endure during difficult times.

To cultivate our true creative power, we have to take a look at where we are right now and how we are evolving and changing. Science is slowly revealing to us that we are on the cusp of a new creative revolution, the likes of which we may never have seen on the planet before. My intention with this book is to help you discover your role in this creative revolution and ways that you can contribute your innate creative genius to the world. I hope this book helps you "re-program" the way you think so that you can realize your true creative genius.

To help you leverage your creative genius and take your place on the leading edge of an evolutionary shift in consciousness, you need to understand some of the clues that scientists are in the middle of interpreting as we begin to paint a bigger picture of what's really up on the planet right now.

1.   Our brains are changing.

According to educational psychologist, author and giftedness expert, Dr. Linda Kreger Silverman, the number of naturally right-brain dominant children began to increase in the late 1970's causing a crisis in the strongly left-brain biased school system.

Right-brain dominant children tend to be visual-spatial learners who master subjects when there is a strong visual and emotional component to how information is presented. Right-brain dominant people see the "big picture" before they discover the "how" and can often wrestle with overwhelm or giant creative impulses that require waiting and experimentation before fulfillment.

They are non-linear, creative thinkers who often have the answer without knowing how they arrived at it and struggle to explain what they know.

As the number of right-brain dominant children increased within the school system, we identified them as dysfunctional and disruptive, giving them labels and diagnoses such as Attention Deficit Disorder (ADD). The number of children diagnosed with ADD skyrocketed in the United States 43 percent between 2003 and 2011, bringing the total number of American children with ADD to nearly 6 million, according to 2015 statistics from the Center for Disease Control and Prevention (CDC). Our response has been—and still is—to medicate many of these cultural creatives, further shutting down our collective access to innovation and creative thinking.

Right brain dominant people are gifted at seeing the relationships between things. Because they see the "big picture", they are able to look at formulas and events and see how seemingly unrelated aspects and pieces are actually key parts of a new whole. They are good at looking at how systems impact each other and often sense possibilities before they know exactly how to make those possibilities a reality. When we only train people to draw on one side of the brain, we lose our ability to really see what other possibilities are available to us.

Silverman also reports that starting in the early 2000's, a new wave of gifted children began to emerge. These children have IQ scores that are immeasurable because the current assessment tools we use do not measure the extent of their intelligence and capacity. This new wave of gifted children are bilaterally dominant in their brain usage, meaning that they use both the right and the left hemisphere of the brain equally, challenging education experts to craft a meaningful and inspiring way to help these adults-of-the-future continue to tap into the full potency of their natural abilities.

The Back to Basics education movement started in the 1970's and led to a heavy focus on the Three R's—reading, writing and arithmetic—minimizing or even excluding the creative arts, ruling them as unnecessary or frivolous components of the educational model. This created a heavy cultural and collective judgment against more than half of our brain's natural creative capacity.

Educational research has recently been pointing us toward the concept that children learn better when information is relevant and integrated. This "new" idea that was once the root of the one-room-schoolhouse has emerged in the current education system as STEM, a way of teaching children that integrates science, technology, engineering and mathematics. This is a nice idea but, again, a heavily left-brained biased way of teaching.

In spite of the growing evidence that the way in which we think and the nature of our intelligence is shifting, the educational system we are conditioned and entrained by is dogmatically adhering to the old way of teaching, making it difficult for sensitive, creative people to cultivate and grow their creative power. Not only is this change in how we think creating large-scale disruption in the education system, it's causing us to have to redefine our collective definition of success.

There is no way of ignoring the fact that the way in which we know how we know is facing an existential crisis.

2. Science is more "accidental" and "improbable" than we are led to believe.

In our eagerness to apply reasoning and science to every aspect of human life, we've gotten confused and even cut ourselves off from our true creative power, limiting our ability to tackle the challenges facing humanity at this crucial time. (As I write this, the Doomsday Clock has been set to 2 minutes to midnight where it hasn't been set since 1953, after the Americans and then the Soviets tested thermonuclear weapons for the first time, within 10 months of each other).

In spite of our rigid adherence to the idea of systems and logic, serendipity and "happy accidents" play a role in 30-50% of scientific discoveries. Scientists themselves often can't explain how "improbable serendipity" influences their scientific discoveries.

Nassim Nicholas Taleb writes in his book, The Black Swan, The Impact of the Highly Improbable[1] that science actually benefits from the chaos of the real world and that uncontrolled aspects of the scientific process increase the possibility of the improbable becoming probable.

If we lock ourselves into the rigid and fixed formulaic ways of thinking that we are so well trained in, we can of-

---

[1]   Taleb, N. N. *The Black Swan: Second Edition: The Impact of the Highly Improbable*, with a new section: "On Robustness and Fragility" (NY: Random House, 2010)

ten miss the blessings of serendipity and so-called luck. Psychologist Alan A. Baumeister[2] claims that sometimes being too scientific and prepared can actually obstruct serendipity, causing scientists to miss the meaning of important accidental discoveries. We also miss the big picture of what's really up on Planet Earth.

According to Dr. Dean Radin[3], senior scientist at the Institute of Noetic Sciences and author of the book, Real Magic, 93 percent of scientists report that they have experienced mystical, spiritual and unexplained phenomenon in their scientific studies, but they hesitate to report it out of fear of losing their research funding.

We can no longer afford to turn a blind eye to serendipity and accidental scientific discoveries and even the power of divine sparks of intuition that reveal answers that reasoning and logical thinking often cannot.

It is no accident that we experience epiphanies and revelations when we are distracted from reasoning and thinking. We often do our best thinking in the shower or when we are at peace. Relaxation and engaging in activities focused on beauty and joy elevate your dopamine levels (a neurotransmitter

---

[2] Baumeister, A.A (1976). "Serendipity and the cerebral localization of pleasure". *Neoplasma*. Department of Psychology, Louisiana State University. **23** (3): 259–63.

[3] Radin, Dean, *Read Magic, Ancient Wisdom, Modern Science, and a Guide to the Secret Power of the Universe,* (Harmony; April 10, 2018)

which increases the experience of pleasure in the brain). Increased dopamine levels actually increase creativity, causing your mind to be able to leap over stuck and fixed understandings and see greater possibilities and expanded relationships between ideas. This is called Fundamental Creativity.

When we are trained to think in ways that are unnatural to our own hard wiring or forcibly exposed to information that many of us feel is uninspiring and disempowering, we shut down access to a higher level of creativity that limits the possibility of what we can create in our own lives and on the planet collectively.

3. **"New" science (Quantum Physics) is presenting us with dilemmas that inevitably are causing us to have to rethink how we know and flipping our entire understanding of creativity on its head.**

The early Scientific Revolution and the Age of Enlightenment, through the works of scientific thinkers, heretics and explorers such as Nicholas Copernicus, Sir Isaac Newton, and Galileo Galilei gave us a consistent set of laws about how the material world operates.

So much of what we know and are taught about how the world works comes from these basic physical laws and understandings. You probably learned the basics of how matter operates when you were in school. You probably also learned that atoms are the building blocks of matter and that everything is made of atoms.

What you might not have learned is that our understanding of the way atoms and subatomic particles behave completely turned the way we interpret the material world on its head.

A new branch of science known as Quantum Physics formally emerged in the 1920s. With the advanced ability to study the atomic world—the building blocks of matter—quantum physicists began to discover that the atomic parts and quantum particles that make up matter behave differently than matter itself and actually break the rules of how matter behaves.

Some of the most notable findings from quantum physics include the fact that when we observe quantum particles, they tend to behave according to how we expect them to behave and that if two different people observe a quantum phenomenon, they will potentially see two different outcomes. In other words, the mere act of observing quantum particles changes the nature of how quantum particles behave.

This has a profound effect on how we experience the material world. Let's look at this concept a little more closely. Imagine for a moment that you are entering a room that is empty except for a chair. If you left the room and your best friend then entered the room to see the same chair, your friend would be looking at a chair that would be slightly different even though no one else was in the room. Of course, it would still be a chair and would pretty much look the same, but scientists can measure subtle changes that would make the chair that your friend notices slightly different.

Why? Because our perspective and observation of matter changes matter's behavior. What quantum physics shows us is that perception does change the experience of reality (although not reality itself).

Let me explain further. Quantum particles move in waves called potentials. It is possible to measure the movement of the wave. But the moment you try to pinpoint the location of a quantum particle on a wave, it stops moving and becomes manifest in form or what quantum physicists call a "collapsed potential" or manifesting. Thus, you can never measure movement and location of quantum particles at the same time. The physical material world is a collection of collapsed quantum potentials.

Quantum physics also added one more big challenge to materialistic understandings of the world. Quantum potentials (waves) of two (or more) related quantum particles can be linked or connected and can influence each other even when they are not physically connected to each other. This is called non-locality.

What that means is that physical experiences and events are not limited to being caused only from physical interactions. The experience of a material phenomenon can be created from a non-local source and that interconnectedness can create influence and impact, even from a distance.

There is obviously much more to quantum physics than these two basic understandings. However, recognizing that perception can alter the experience of reality and that the experience of reality itself is subjective forces us to have to examine our understanding of scientific facts a little more closely and redefine many of our previous thought forms about cause, effect, and reality.

Quantum physics calls on us to become more conscious of the nature of our perceptions and to consciously cultivate perceptions that expand, rather than limit, our awareness of potential answers to our challenges. When we think about what IS possible and engage our creative imaginations rather than shutting down the power of our creative thinking with doubt and suspicion, we may find that we see more possibilities, greater answers, and elegant solutions that purely linear thinking may rule out.

The power to change our perception is also the power to change the nature of the reality we are living. If you change your perception and consequently change your reality AND the changes you make impact the people who you are locally and non-locally connected to, then it makes sense that individual shifts in perspective can ultimately begin to dramatically change the nature of our collective reality as well.

Creativity is not just being artsy. It is the ability to deliberately collapse quantum potentials into your reality by consciously leveraging your perspective. In other words, you create your own reality, which then adds to the reality of others. If you want to create the reality you want to be living, you have to start with what I believe is the most fundamental creative question you can ask yourself: Who is the YOU who is creating your reality?

When we know who we are and how our perception of ourselves is programming the experiences we are having, we can begin to define who we are to match the reality - and the elegant solutions - we are seeking.

4. Our experience of collective reality is a phenomenon of the evolution of consciousness.

The nature of life is growth, expansion and evolution.

Our personal perception of reality creates our experience of reality, including the experience of our current understanding of scientific principles. The nature of our perception is evolving based on where we are in our growth cycle. Think about it. How you see the world today is very different from how you saw the world as a child. You've grown and evolved a lot since then. Humanity itself has also grown and evolved, changing our collective perspectives over time.

Our collective perception of reality is also changing depending on our collective growth and evolution. The more humanity learns and evolves, the more our understandings of the world change and grow along with us. Before the Scientific Revolution, our understanding of the world was influenced by mystery, anecdotal evidence, and superstition. As our collective consciousness evolved, we began to change the way we understood the world. Our ability to organize information and see relationships changed.

The way in which we perceive the world is a benchmark for where we are in collective consciousness. As we change and grow together, so does our collective understanding of the world. What that means is that our scientific understanding of how the world works is a manifestation of our collective consciousness. We can plot the growth of consciousness by looking at how the way in which we understand the way the world works has changed.

The Scientific Revolution gave us truths about how the material world functions. These understandings were a function of what I'll call Material Consciousness.

Hallmarks of Material Thinking and Consciousness include

- Finite amounts and solutions
- Fixed laws with probable, possible, and predictable results
- Formulas
- Reasoning
- Logic
- Nature and Natural Law
- A drive for "certainty"
- A sense of value rooted in materialism

O   Situationally creative (Reactive)

With the advent of Quantum Science in the 1900s, we saw a shift in the expansion of consciousness. I'll call this Quantum Consciousness.

Hallmarks of Quantum Consciousness include:

O   The idea that your "thoughts create your reality"
O   We are all connected by virtue of the Quantum Field (the energy field where all potentials are stored)
O   We create non-locally, not just through physical action
O   Fundamental Creativity (inspiration that bypasses conditioning)
O   A drive towards well-being instead of material gain
O   Embracing change, uncertainty, and potential
O   Value based on quality and energy, not just material measurement

The New Thought movement that emerged simultaneously with the delineation of Quantum Physics as a stand-alone field of study included the teachings of thought leaders including Ernest Holmes, Edgar Cayce, Madame Blavatsky, Rudolf Steiner, Neville Goddard, and Maria Montessori. The book Think and Grow Rich by Napoleon Hill was published in 1937, a remarkably "quantum" title for a book that explored the importance of mindset and success.

We saw Cubism and Surrealism and other styles of "mind-bending" artistic expression bursting onto the scene during this time, created by artists including Pablo Picasso and Salvador Dali, who sought to skew our perceptions to a new way of thinking and seeing reality.

As the last century of science has unfolded, we have discovered that evolution itself may be more conscious and deliberate than we thought. The work of Rupert Sheldrake, who pioneered the idea of morphogenetic fields—conscious fields of energy that drive the evolutionary process and create energy templates for creation prior to manifestation in the material world—has turned the field of evolutionary biology upside down.

We've seen research by thought leaders including Lynne McTaggart, Dawson Church, Dean Radin, and many others that has demonstrated in scientifically valid ways the theory that thoughts, intentions, and even prayers can influence what we experience. We can create matter and change the nature of random events simply by consciously applying the energy of the mind.

We are looking at the emergence of an economy that is no longer exclusively driven by material gain and that people are seeking better quality of life, more well-being, and fulfillment versus accumulation of possessions and money. Note the new trends towards minimalism and the Tiny House Movement.

We are changing the nature of what and how we eat. Many of us are no longer willing to eat in a way that creates pain for other sentient beings. We are driven to eat in a way that reflects our consciousness, in a way that is sustainable and promotes peace.

All of this is relatively new on the human timeline but marks an important surge in the evolution of consciousness. As we stand on the brink of this powerful creative revolution, the clues about what is next for humanity and how to get there lies in our evolving understanding of the material world and how we create and influence our experience of it.

Your lesson for this chapter can be found here:

CHAPTER 2

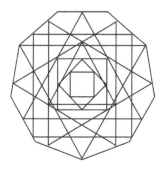

The Mechanics of Creating

Each new generation is the culmination of the whole of evolution. We are born on the leading edge of consciousness. You are here at this vital time because you are a part of the shift that is happening on the planet right now. The work you do on your own personal growth and expansion is essential to the evolution of the world.

The ways in which we create and the drivers for what we create on the planet are changing. Most of us learned that to create success in the world we had to work hard. We measured success with numbers. Our personal value was gauged on how much material value we had earned. We learned that if you want "more" you have to work harder.

There were "formulas" for success. You set goals. You work hard. You fight for your share.

In the last 30 years, we began to play with the idea that there was more to creating than just sheer will and effort. The idea that your thoughts create your reality began to take hold and gain traction in the mainstream. In 2006, the documentary *The Secret* was released and the verb "manifest" became part of our cultural conversation. Vision boards, positive thinking and affirmations were incorporated as part of goal-setting strategies for creating. (You could even buy *The Secret's* companion book at Walmart!)

The story of Human Design tells us that our energy field and the way we interact with the material world is about to go through a major upgrade. We are on the edge of a Creative Revolution. Our bodies and our DNA are evolving to hold higher frequencies of energy that support a shift in our ability to create.

We are learning to consciously harness frequencies of energy and manifest in the world in alignment with the frequencies we hold. We are breaking free from material consciousness rooted in binary thinking and finite resources that have to be gathered through hard labor. We are learning to create with the power of our minds, hearts, and consciousness in a new way that will help us find the solutions to the challenges facing humanity.

Success in this new world will be measured by quality of life, not numbers. Your success will be measured not only in how much well-being you cultivate for yourself, but also in how much well-being you add to the world.

You are an essential part of this story. Your own shift in consciousness and the work you do to heal the karma of your own sense of value initiates a code of energy that has the power to lift others. The energy frequency you carry as you heal yourself reverberates in your community, impacts those you love and anyone you connect with. Your personal evolution changes the world around you.

As more and more people have access to higher frequencies of energy, the more this evolutionary shift is transmitted. This is the key to unlocking our evolutionary code of ascension and healing the pain of a planet trapped in chronic trauma cycles; cycles that have resulted in people forgetting their unique, vital, and irreplaceable role in the world as well as their true creative potential.

We are not victims of our reality living our lives without choice or influence over what happens. We are co-creators of this world, translating divine inspiration into action and third-dimensional form. Our thoughts, our conditioning and our lives are, in essence, a giant feedback loop for the expansion of consciousness in manifested form.

If we are going to change the nature of reality on this planet and create a world of equitable, sustainable peace, then we have to heal ourselves first. Each and every one of us carries the seed for the potential of this shift. The more we elevate our own frequency of energy as a result of our own healing, the more we are able to seed the energy of integrity and alignment into the world.

The more we de-condition ourselves from the stories we've been telling that limit who we are and our creative potential, the more we create choice over how we're going to experience the shift on the planet. The work you do creates choice, not only for yourself but also for the world.

We are standing on the brink of a powerful choice point on the planet. The evolution we face is inevitable, but we have to choose how we are going to evolve. We have the potential to claw, fight and scramble our way to our evolution, or we can heal, align and peacefully shift the world, one conscious thought and action at a time.

To understand what's going on in this shift we're experiencing, we have to start with some basic assumptions about how we create and experience the material world. We're going to start by looking at the basic parts of the "creative equation" and the mechanics of how we manifest the experience of the lives we're living.

Quantum Physics

In the early 1900s, a powerful new field of science, Quantum Physics, was recognized as an official branch of physics. Quantum Physicists study the building blocks of matter - atoms and the smaller particles that make up the elements of the material world.

Quantum Physicists realized early on that the building blocks of matter don't act in the same way we know matter to behave. Specifically, they began to discover that the act of observing quantum particles actually affects how the quantum particles behave. Expectation influences the experience of reality.

In a study reported in the February 26, 1998, issue of *Nature*[4] researchers at the Weizmann Institute of Science

---

[4]   Weizmann Institute of Science. Nature, February 26, 1998 (Vol. 391, pp. 871-874)

conducted a highly controlled experiment demonstrating how a beam of electrons is affected by the act of being observed. The experiment revealed that the greater the amount of "watching", the greater the observer's influence on what actually takes place.

Quantum Physicists also noted that they could either measure the movement of a quantum particle wave (a "potential") or they could measure the location of a quantum particle but never both at the same time.

Potentials are not made manifest until we observe them. The location or "manifestation" of a quantum particle, turning potential into matter, is influenced by our observation and our expectation of its behavior. When we observe a potential wave of quantum particles, they transform from a state of potential to a state of material manifestation.

Let's translate that into practical understanding. Your life is filled with potential. The story of who you are is a collection of innumerable potentials, most of which you won't manifest into reality simply because life is too short for you to fulfill all the options available to you! Your current reality is a collection of the potentials that you have made manifest. The meanings we hold about the elements of our life influence which moving waves of potential we materialize into our physical reality.

Imagine for a moment that you are swimming in a sea of potentials. A potential is essentially a neutral concept - an archetype - one that has the possibility to be fulfilled in many different ways. Your perception and the meanings you have about a potential determine how you experience that potential in your life.

Let's look at a specific example. Close your eyes for a moment and think of the word "creativity."

Creativity, in this sea of potentials you are swimming in, is a neutral concept. Creativity is simply the ability to create something.

How you perceive the idea of creativity, your experiences of being creative in your life, and the beliefs you are conditioned by, influence how you manifest the potential of creativity in your life.

Let's say you, like all children, were born with a deep connection to your natural creative ability. You spent your free time daydreaming and thinking about all the things you'd love to do with your life. One day, while you were in school, you were looking out the window and dreaming about what it would be like to ride a horse when the teacher came by, took her ruler and banged it loudly on your desk, startling you out of your creative daydream.

This experience left you so startled, that you made a conscious choice to not dream in school again, shutting down a core element of your creative power. (You also never gave yourself permission to ride a horse in your life…).

In your family of origin, you grew up with parents who were practical, who believed that all dreams were born of hard work, and that if you want to do fun, creative things with your life, you have to earn them after you get your work done first. Creativity was a luxury, and in your family, it was a luxury you couldn't afford. Your family's work ethic entrained you to put your dreams on the back burner with the hopes that someday you'd earn the right to manifest them into reality.

At sixteen years of age, you fell in love with literature. You'd always been a voracious reader, but as you matured and you began to really understand the elegance and power of the written word, you decided that you'd like to become a professional writer.

When you shared your dream with your father, he scolded you for being impractical, informed you if you majored in literature in college that he wouldn't pay your tuition and that you'd better pick a more profitable and practical career path if you wanted to get anywhere in your life.

You compromised, majored in education, and got a job teaching school. Now, as an adult, anytime you think about pursuing your passion, creating what you really want in your life and the prospect of fulfilling your creative urges, you push those desires down. Sometimes you think about writing when you retire. In your daily life, you never give yourself the gift of fulfilling the full expression of your creativity.

All of these experiences coupled with the collective consciousness around the idea of creativity that you grew up with are carried in your mental and emotional body - where you hold the memories that make up the narrative you are telling yourself about your creativity and your creative power.

This is the filter through which you observe and perceive the potential of creativity in the Quantum Field. Your filter is influencing how you manifest creativity in your life.

Instead of telling yourself a story about your innate creative ability when you allow yourself to dream about your dream of being a writer, you shut down your connection to your dream because your filter won't allow you to even entertain it as a possibility. Consequently, you never manifest the possibility of fulfilling that dream in your reality.

The New Thought Movement, which started in the early 19th century around the same time that Quantum Physics gained recognition as an official branch of physics, seeded the collective consciousness with the idea that your thoughts create your reality.

Our deeper understanding of genetics, neurobiology, and peak potential activation has demonstrated that there is more to creating your reality than your thoughts, but that at its core, the idea that YOU create your reality is true.

In order to gain influence over your experience of reality you have to know how your mental and emotional body filter is conditioned. Who is the you who is creating your reality and what parts of your you might you need to realign in order to create the reality you want?

Human Design refers to the idea that we are all conditioned to be who we think we are. In this next section I want to explore the idea of conditioning and many of the factors that go into forming your current personal narrative - the narrative that is influencing what you choose to create out of the Quantum Field.

There are five key areas of conditioning:

1. Openness in the Human Design Chart

Traditional Human Design teaches that the centers that you have open (white) on your chart receive and amplify energy and information from the world around you. The energy you are receiving is amplified and experienced intensely. When you are in a consistent energy field, such as in your family of origin where you experienced the same energy for your entire childhood, it's easy to confuse the energy of others as your own.

This confusion causes us to engage in predictable behavioral patterns that become coping mechanisms for managing the intensity of the energy that we experience in our openness. The intensity of the energy causes us to identify with it and we form an identity around our openness. We think we have energy that does not belong to us.

Let's say, for example, that you have an open Emotional Solar Plexus. That means that you take in other people's emotional energy and you amplify it. If you grew up in a family that has an aura of a defined Emotional Solar Plexus, then you grew up in an energy field that always held emotional energy. As a person with an open Emotional Solar Plexus, you amplified that emotional energy and, because you experienced this intense energy configuration over the span of your childhood, you may have grown up thinking you are a dramatic and emotional person, when, according to your Human Design configuration, you are not.

2. Imprinting

Your Human Design chart represents the mechanics of how you interface with the world, but your life experience informs you as to how you utilize these mechanics.

Our neurobiology plays an important role in the formation of who we are. We are not only imprinted by the energy field in which we grew up; we are imprinted by our parents' behaviors, their belief systems and our family culture. A big part of your identity is based on what you learned from watching and being imprinted by your family.

This imprinting influences how you respond to stress, what you eat, what you believe, your level of physical fitness, your self-talk, your resilience, and more. We cannot escape the need to explore our family of origin and how they influenced our life choices if we are going to de-condition ourselves.

3. Intergenerational Family Dynamics

Human Design shows us that we inherit our unique energy configuration from our grandparents. This sets us up for the potential of long-term intergenerational dynamics that cause us to live out different sides of the same family interaction over and over again, both as parents and as children.

If we are energetically similar to our grandparents, that means that our parents had to confront similar energy themes that they experienced from their own parents through us as their children. We, in turn, have to deal with the same "replay" of energy themes through our own journey as parents and so on and so on...

Let's say, for example, your family had a dynamic that included the Gate 21, the Gate of Self-Regulation. The Gate 21 often has a relationship dynamic that involves controlling or feeling controlled.

If your grandparents carried this theme in their chart, your mother may have struggled with feeling controlled by her parents. In response, your mother may have adopted a very permissive parenting style. If you carry the Gate 21 in your own chart, you may have experienced this energy as a deep need for structure, consistency and rules to feel safe and valued.

If your mother's permissive parenting style left you with too much freedom and a need for better boundaries and structure, you might go on to be too controlling or rigid with your own children, setting your family up to repeat the inter-generational theme of control.

When we heal the more painful aspect of these inter-generational family dynamics and learn to live out the higher potential of the interaction between the configurations in our family energy constellation, we have the potential to not only heal our own wounds but to shift the dynamic in our families for generations to come.

4. Genetics

Your DNA, the gene code carried inside your cells, influences many aspects of who you are and who you think you are. There are certain aspects of your personality that are part of your genetic structure.

Your DNA is much more malleable than you probably were taught in school. Protein coats on our DNA called epigenes control the expression and regulation of our genes. Epigenes contain information about our environment. They also can hold information about the environment and experiences of our ancestors. Your ancestral "memories" are stored on an epigenetic level and can influence how some of your gene code is activated or de-activated.

For example, in 2015, Dr. Rachel Yehuda[55], director of Traumatic Stress Studies at the Mount Sinai School of Medicine found that the children of the survivors of the Holocaust had epigenetic changes to a gene that was linked to their levels of cortisol, a hormone involved in the stress response. This epigenetic change made these people more vulnerable to anxiety disorders and a generalized stress response to life.

Even your epigenetic profile is malleable. Simple lifestyle changes, diet, exercise, and even consciously changing the thoughts you have, can shift your genetic programming and, again, change the nature of what you pass down to generations to come.

5. The Personality Crystal, the Design Crystal and the Magnetic Monopole

Human Design adds a few other components to the creative equation that help us deepen our understanding of how we create and the story of who we think we are. In order to understand these key players in the creative equation, we have to go back to the moment of your conception.

---

5   Yehuda, R., Kahana, B., Southwick, S. M., & Giller, E. L. (1976, January 01). Depressive features in holocaust survivors with post-traumatic stress disorder. Retrieved December 11, 2020, from https://link.springer.com/article/10.1007/BF02103016

Our life and soul purpose are encoded in two crystalline bodies of energy called the Design Crystal and the Personality Crystal. These aren't actual physical crystals but codes of information that help define who you are in this lifetime. At the moment of your conception, your father's energy calls forth a crystalline code of energy that resides in the earth. This crystalline code of energy, called the Design Crystal, contains the code for your human life story and purpose. It initiates and manages the process of the development of your body as you grow from undifferentiated cells into a baby. The Design Crystal carries your gene codes, your epigenetic programming, your ancestral memories, and all the things that make your unique human story.

The Design Crystal is bundled with a special magnet, called the Magnetic Monopole. The Magnetic Monopole is a magnetic force that only attracts. Your Magnetic Monopole is encoded with the information that will attract into your life all the experiences you are destined to have that are essential to your life story. The Magnetic Monopole is also the source of the Law of Attraction.

The events in your life that have seemed fated or part of an unavoidable destiny are encoded in your Magnetic Monopole. As we evolve, our ability to consciously program our monopole is growing and we are gaining more control over what we attract into our lives.

The third component, the Personality Crystal, contains the code for your soul purpose. It enters the body at the moment of your birth.

At birth, the Design Crystal takes up residence in the Ajna Center. The Magnetic Monopole resides in the Identity Center, and the Personality Crystal is located in the Head Center.

The combination of the Design Crystal, the Personality Crystal, and the Magnetic Monopole help define the field of choices you are choosing from over the course of your life. Obviously, the full range of potentials of what you can choose for your life is quite large and you certainly won't run out of options in what you create in your reality! This limitation of options is important because it helps define who you perceive yourself to be in your current incarnation.

This combination of codes also makes you a unique once-in-a-lifetime cosmic event!

Most of what you think about who you are is based on your conditioning and what you carry in your mental and emotional body. The meanings you hold about ideas and potentials influence how they manifest in your physical reality.

The most important thing you can do right now to support the creation of an equitable, sustainable, and peaceful world is to begin a systematic exploration of the meanings you hold about who you are, why you're here, and what you're capable of. The biggest part of our work at this time, as volunteers here to birth this new world, is to untangle humanity from old collective and personal beliefs about lack and limitation.

Our Human Design shows us that the highest potential expression of humanity is rooted in Love. We are designed to love ourselves, love each other and to create from a deep connection to a loving spiritual Source. This is true for all of us personally and collectively.

But we can't bring this ideal into form if our perception of who we are - our "filter" - doesn't support this as a possibility that we choose within the Quantum Field. If we don't hold a narrative creating an identity that is infinitely loving, that believes in the possibility of equitable, sustainable and just peace, we can't manifest love on the planet.

The most important thing we can each do right now to midwife the birth of a new world is to align our personal identity with the true story of who we really are. We must consciously and deliberately inventory our identity, heal past traumas that are keeping us stuck in stories and meanings that are less than who we can be, and reclaim our personal value.

Your personal journey of de-conditioning is the key to unlocking the evolution of consciousness on the planet. As you heal and align yourself, you transmit a frequency of energy that unlocks the hearts of others. Higher frequencies of energy modulate lower frequencies and lift them up, opening doorways for new potentials to manifest in the world.

The evolution of the world is inevitable. The code for the transformation of humanity is already complete. The challenge we are facing now is determining how we are going to translate that code into action.

With old collective beliefs rooted in lack, "not enoughness" and fear, the meanings we hold have the potential to craft an evolutionary journey that is rooted in war, poverty, hoarding, and more, making the road to our evolution rocky and frightening.

If we shift these old meanings and beliefs, starting first with ourselves, we have the power to change the quality of the journey we are on. We can accelerate and amplify the potential for a gentle shift in the story of humanity, creating an easy transition to sufficiency and support for every sentient being on the planet in the fastest, most enduring way possible.

We will evolve. That part is certain.

The question is how are we going to get to where we're going? When enough of us generate meanings and beliefs that support the idea - the dream - of a sustainable, equitable, and peaceful world, we change the "filter" through which we choose potentials and we begin the process of manifesting the New World in a gentle and easy way.

The work you do on a personal level, the act of re-writing the personal narrative you tell about who you are, might not seem revolutionary. However, it is the most vital work we must do on the planet at this time to build a critical mass of high-frequency energy that will usher in the transformation and shifts we need to activate to create a peaceful transition to a new world of peace.

Exploration:

Take some time to contemplate or journal about the following questions. Your answers are simply giving you insights into what meanings you may be holding right now. Notice your answers with loving curiosity and without judgment. This is simply a series of questions designed to give you awareness. Awareness is the first step to transformation.

1. What meanings do you hold about peace on the planet? Do you believe that peace is possible?
2. How are you creating peace in your personal life? Are you peaceful? What old beliefs do you have about fighting, getting your share, setting boundaries? How do these beliefs manifest in your life?
3. What meanings do you have about sharing? Do you think there are enough resources to share in the world? Do you experience fear about giving too much? Do you share freely? Do you hoard?

4. Do you trust Source? Do you believe you are enough? Do you believe that you are supported? Do you think you can always be supported?

Your lesson for this chapter can be found here:

CHAPTER 3

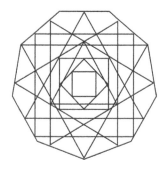

The Evolving Heart

To get the most understanding out of this chapter, I want to invite you to suspend any previous scientific knowledge that you have about evolution, most of which you probably learned in a high school biology class at some point. Much of what we have been taught about evolution is based on Darwinian evolution, a theory that has, at best, a lot of holes in it.

Evolution may be much more intentional and conscious than we were taught in school. The assumption that I'd like you to make is that the experience of our current reality is the manifestation of the evolution of consciousness - not our physical form. Evolution of our physical form is a manifestation of an evolution of consciousness first!

We are in a cosmic feedback loop. As consciousness experiences itself through us and our earthly experience, it evolves. Our experience on the planet, including how we understand life, the material world, the world of work, science, medicine, creativity, and more is the result consciousness. The more consciousness evolves through our experience of the world, the more our experience of reality changes.

In traditional Human Design, Ra taught that we have "no choice." There is some truth to that statement. We have no choice as to whether we will evolve. Evolution is inevitable.

We also have "no choice" when we are conditioned and disconnected from our authentic selves. If we merely live from the imprinting of experience of our lives and disconnect from the heart of who we are, we react to the unfolding of the cosmic plan and lose our ability to consciously serve the evolution of humanity.

If we remember our true identity and we engage with life consciously, we absolutely have choice over how we experience life and we can use the feedback loop to gauge our growth and expansion and serve the creation of a peaceful new world.

You may not be able to stop the unfolding of the evolution of consciousness, but you have total control over how you're going to experience the world. The question we are dealing with collectively is not what are we evolving towards, but rather how we are going to get there.

We are headed toward creating a world of equitable, sustainable peace. That endpoint is set, as you'll see when we explore the changes that we are facing through the shifts in the Human Design chart. We will either evolve in a joyful, conscious, and aligned way, or we will fight and destroy the old world (and maybe each other) before we emerge into the new.

It's up to us.

We have to first explore where we've been in order to understand where we're headed and how to influence our experience of the changes ahead.

From 7 Centers to 9 Centers

A vital change in the human energy field occurred during our current Human Design global cycle, a cycle that started in 1615. This major evolutionary change set the stage for the upcoming cycle in human evolution that will begin in 2027.

In 1781, our internal and energetic hard wiring shifted. During this major change, we changed from being a 7-centered energy being to being a 9-centered energy being.

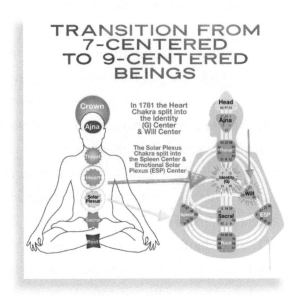

The Human Design centers in the chart are derived from the seven chakras in the Hindu Chakra System. A chakra (translated as a "spinning wheel of energy") processes different kinds of energy and is related to specific human archetypal and energy themes. The split from 7 centers to 9 centers brought with it a new kind of inner authority that helped humanity liberate itself from outer authoritarian structures. It also gave us a new drive to explore and define our material world beyond old religious and superstitious beliefs.

The change in the energy field in 1781 was the manifestation of hundreds of years of humanity working diligently to understand the material world. This major change came at the heels of the scientific revolution and resulted in ways of thinking that were grounded in reasoning, linear thinking and logic.

In 1781, the Heart Chakra, the chakra responsible for self-love, altruism, generosity, kindness, and respect, split into two centers, the Identity Center and the Will Center.

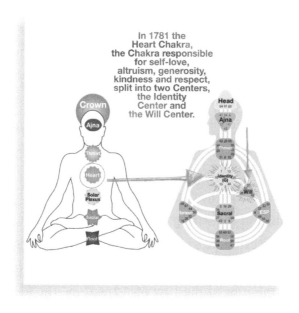

The Identity Center

The Identity Center is the center for love and life direction in the Human Design chart. This important evolutionary change in the chart dramatically augmented the story of the heart of humanity and gave us the power to consciously calibrate the direction our life takes us based on the quality of love we are experiencing in our lives.

According to the Institute of HeartMath, "The heart is the most powerful generator of electromagnetic energy in the human body, producing the largest rhythmic electromagnetic field of any of the body's organs." From Human Design, we know that the electromagnetic resonance field is generated by the Magnetic Monopole located in the Identity Center.

One of the key components in the human creative process is the Magnetic Monopole. Your thoughts create neurotransmitters, biochemicals that produce an emotional response. In response to neurotransmitter production, you produce an emotional frequency of energy. This frequency of energy calibrates the Magnetic Monopole to attract experiences into your life that match your emotions, your perception of yourself, and the degree to which you love yourself.

This shift in the wiring of the heart gave us the power to consciously calibrate the Magnetic Monopole. This expansion of our creative potential and sovereignty over our own life path is the root of the Law of Attraction. The idea that "your thoughts create your reality" is a big surge forward towards the evolution of Quantum Creativity and the expansion of our human creative potential.

Who we are - our identity - rooted in our personal narrative, gives us direction in life. The story we tell about who we are, and the feelings generated in response to those thoughts programs the magnetic resonance field of the heart originating through the Magnetic Monopole.

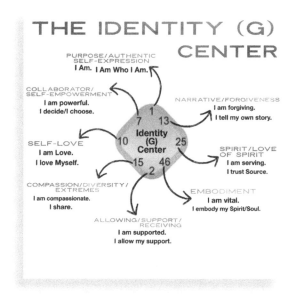

The gates of the Identity Center, where the Magnetic Monopole is located, give us a code that helps guide us in creating deep alignment with the original intention for our life. Our higher purpose is encoded into the Identity Center. The gates of the Identity Center help us unlock the energies necessary for us to fulfill the full potential of our life and soul purpose.

Our evolutionary mission on the planet at this time is to consciously use the codes of the Identity Center to transmit frequencies of love on the planet. The gates of the Identity Center tell us the code for the kind of love we need to cultivate in order to align with our authentic identity: loving be-ings in human form.

Below is a list of each of the gates of the Identity Cen-ter and contemplations for you to explore the meanings you hold around each of these themes. It does not matter wheth-er you have these energies defined or open in your chart. We all have all of these energies. We just experience them differ-ently depending on our unique hardwiring.

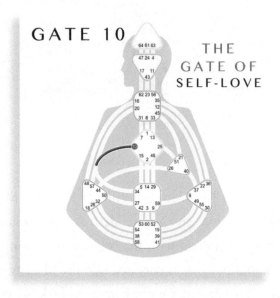

Gate 10 - The Gate of Self-Love

Challenge: To learn to love yourself. To learn to take respon-sibility for your own creations.

Mastery: To see your love for yourself as the source of your true creative power.

Unbalanced Expression: To question your lovability, struggle to prove your worthiness of love to give up and settle for less than what you deserve and to blame others for your circumstances and situations. Victim consciousness.

Contemplations:

Do you love yourself?

What can you do to deepen your self-love?

Where can you find evidence of your lovability in your life right now?

What do you need to do to take responsibility for situations you hate in your life right now?

What needs to change?

Where are you holding blame or victimhood in your life? How could you turn that energy around?

AFFIRMATION:

I am an individuated aspect of the Divine. I am born of Love. My nature is to love and be loved. I am in the full flow of giving and receiving love. I know that the quality of love that I have for myself sets the direction for what I attract into my life. I am constantly increasing the quality of love I experience and share with the world.

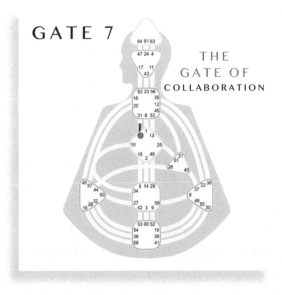

GATE 7

THE
GATE OF
COLLABORATION

Gate 7 - The Gate of Collaboration

Challenge: To master the need to be in front and allow yourself to serve through building teams, collaborating, and influencing the figurehead of leadership. To be at peace with serving the leader through support and collaboration. To recognize that the voice of the leader is only as strong and powerful as the support they receive.

Mastery: To embrace that power comes from supporting, influencing and collaborating with leadership. To recognize that you don't have to be the figurehead to influence the direction that leadership assumes. The chief of staff is often more powerful than the president. The energy to unify people around an idea that influences the direction of leadership.

Unbalanced Expression: To struggle and fight to be seen and recognized as *the* leader at cost to your energy and the fulfillment of your purpose.

Contemplations:

What are you gifts and strengths? How do you use those gifts to influence and lead others?

How do you feel about not being the figurehead of leadership? What happens when you "only" support the leadership? Do you still feel powerful? Influential?

Make a list of the times when your influence has positively directed leadership.

AFFIRMATION:

I am an agent of peace who influences the direction and organization of leadership. I unify people around ideas. I influence with my wisdom, my knowledge and my connections. I am a team builder, a collaborator, and I organize people in ways that empower them and support them in creating a collective direction rooted in compassion.

GATE 1

THE
GATE OF
PURPOSE

Gate 1 - The Gate of Purpose

Challenge: To discover a personal, meaningful and world-changing narrative that aligns with a sense of purpose and mission. "I am..." To learn to love yourself enough to honor the idea that your life is the canvas and you are the artist. What you create with your life IS the contribution you give the world.

Mastery: The ability to know the Authentic Self and a deep connection with a life purpose.

Unbalanced Expression: An erratic or purposeless life, panic and a feeling of "failing" at a life mission, pressure to create something unique in the world, struggle to find purpose, hiding because the purpose feels too big, too much, or egotistical.

Contemplations:

Are you fully expressing your authentic self?

What needs to be healed, released, aligned, or brought to your awareness for you to more deeply express your authentic self?

Where are you already expressing who you are?

Where have you settled or compromised? What needs to change?

Do you feel connected to your life purpose? What do you need to do to deepen that connection?

AFFIRMATION:

My life is an integral part of the cosmos and the divine plan. I honor my life and know that the full expression of who I am is the purpose of my life. The more I am who I am, the more I create a frequency of energy that supports others in doing the same. I commit to exploring all of who I am.

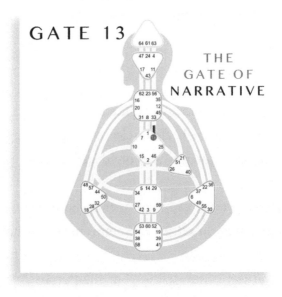

GATE 13

THE
GATE OF
NARRATIVE

Gate 13 - The Gate of Narrative

Challenge: To forgive the past and redefine who you are each and every day. To tell a personal narrative that is empowering, self-loving and reflects your value and your authentic self. To bear witness to the pain and narrative of others and offer them a better story that allows them to expand on their abundance and blessings.

Mastery: The ability to use the power of personal narrative to create with power and intention.

Unbalanced Expression: Staying stuck in old stories. Holding on to old past pains. Staying the victim in a story that repeats itself because your personal narrative is stuck in an old story.

Contemplations:

What stories about your life are you holding on to?

Do these stories reflect who you really are and what you really want to be creating with your life?

What or who do you need to forgive in order to liberate yourself to tell a new story?

What secrets or stories are you holding for others? Do you need to release them?

Write the true story of who you really are...

AFFIRMATION:

The story that I tell myself and the world of who I am sets the tone and the direction for my life. I am the artist and creator of my story. I have the power to rewrite my story every day. The true story I tell from my heart allows me to serve my right place in the cosmic plan.

GATE 25

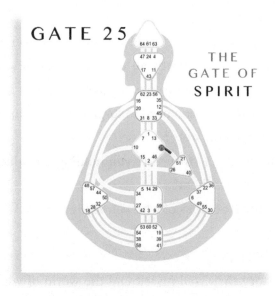

THE
GATE OF
SPIRIT

Gate 25 - The Gate of Spirit

Challenge: To trust the divine order in all of your life. To learn to connect with Source as the path to creating wellbeing in your life. To remember that your life serves an irreplaceable role in the cosmic plan and to honor that role and to live from it. To trust Source.

Mastery: To connect with Source with consistency and diligence so as to fulfill your divine purpose and fulfill the true story of who you are and the role you play in the cosmic plan. To use your alignment with Source as a way of healing the world.

Unbalanced Expression: Fear and mistrust of Spirit. Using your life strictly for personal gains regardless of the impact on others. Ego in the lowest expression. Not feeling worthy of being loved by Source and using your willpower to create instead of align.

Contemplations:

Do you trust Source?

Do you have a regular practice that connects you to Source?

Do you know your life purpose? Are you living true to your purpose? How can you deepen your connection to your purpose?

AFFIRMATION:

I am an agent of the divine. My life is the fulfillment of divine order and the cosmic plan. When I am connected to Source, I serve my right place. I take up no more than my space and no less than my place in the world. I serve, and through serving, I am supported.

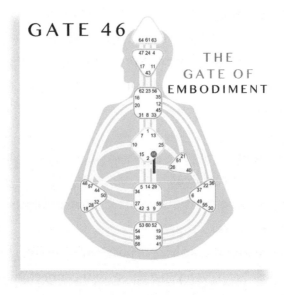

GATE 46

THE
GATE OF
EMBODIMENT

Gate 46 - The Gate of Embodiment

Challenge: To learn to love your body. To learn to fully be in your body. To learn to love the sensual nature of your physical form and to move it with love and awareness.

Mastery: To recognize that the body is the vehicle for the soul and to love the body as a vital element of the soul's expression in life. To nurture, be grounded in and fully care for the body. To savor the physicality of the human experience. To explore how to fully embody the spirit in your body and to be committed and devoted to seeing how much life force you can embody into your physical form.

Unbalanced Expression: To disconnect from the body. To hate the body. To avoid nurturing or taking care of the body. To avoid the commitments and consistency necessary to fully embody life force. To hide or disfigure the body.

Contemplations:

Do you love your body? What can you do to deepen your love for your body?

What parts of your body do you love and appreciate? Make a list of every part of your body that you love.

What do you need to do to amplify the life force you are experiencing in your body?

What kinds of devotion and commitment do you experience that help you harness greater amounts of life force in your body?

How can you deepen your commitment and devotion to your body?

AFFIRMATION:

My body is the vehicle for my soul. My ability to fully express who I am – and my life and soul purpose – is deeply rooted in my body's ability to carry my soul. I love, nurture and commit to my body. I appreciate all of its miraculous abilities and form. Every day I love my body more.

GATE 2

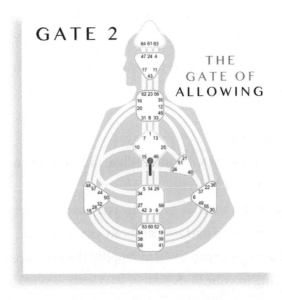

THE
GATE OF
ALLOWING

Gate 2 - The Gate of Allowing

Challenge: To love yourself enough to open to the flow of support, love, and abundance. To incrementally increase over the course of your life what you're willing to allow yourself to receive. To learn to know that you are valuable and lovable simply because you exist.

Mastery: To set intentions and move solidly towards the fulfillment of the Authentic Self with complete trust that you are supported in being the full expression of who you are and your life purpose, even if you don't know how or what the support will look like. Trust in Source. Living in a state of gratitude.

Unbalanced Expression: To experience stress, fear, and ultimately compromise on what you want and who you are because you don't trust that you are supported. To be valiantly self-sufficient to the point of burning yourself out. To never ask for help.

Contemplations:

Do you ask for help when you need it? Why or why not?

Do you trust the Universe/God/Spirit/Source to support you in fulfilling your intentions?

Are you grateful for what you have? Make a list of everything you're grateful for.

Can you transform your worry into trust?

Do you believe that you deserve to be supported?

AFFIRMATION:

I allow myself to receive the full flow of resources and abundance I need to fully express all of who I am. I recognize that my life is a vital, irreplaceable part of the cosmic tapestry and I receive all that I need because it helps me contribute all that I am.

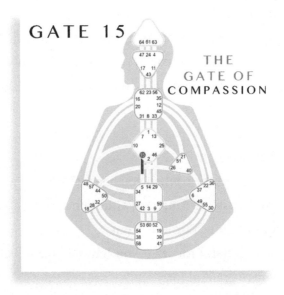

GATE 15

THE GATE OF COMPASSION

Gate 15 - The Gate of Compassion

Challenge: To learn to allow yourself to be in the flow of your own rhythm. To not beat yourself up because you don't have daily "habits". To have the courage to do the right thing even if you are worried about not having enough. To share from the heart without giving up your heart and serving as a martyr.

Mastery: The ability to trust your own flow and rhythm, to trust that you will have cycles that disrupt old patterns and force you to re-create your direction and flow. To learn to set parameters for your creativity and work when it feels right and then rest in between. Nature has rhythm AND extremes.

You are here to change old rhythms and patterns to align them with greater compassion.

Unbalanced Expression: Self-judgment and extreme habits that are frenetic and non-productive. Trying to force your natural waves of rhythm into the daily practices and habits that society defines as successful and struggling with follow-through. Denying your own heart. Being too afraid to do what feels right.

Contemplations:
Do you trust your own rhythm?
Do you share from the Heart? Do you overshare? Does your sharing compromise your own heart?
Do you judge your own rhythm? Can you find peace in aligning with your own rhythm?
What old patterns do you need to break?

AFFIRMATION:
Like the power of a hurricane to transform the shoreline, my unique rhythm brings change to the landscape of my life and the world around me. I embrace my own rhythm and acknowledge the power of my own heart. I share with ease and I serve my own heart as the foundation of all I have to give the world. I bring alignment with compassion in all that I am.

The Will Center

The shift from seven centers to nine centers also gave us a profound new perspective on our personal self. The Will Center, also referred to as the Ego, is the center that, in traditional Human Design, interprets value on the material plane. The Will Center is also a motor, the seat of "will power" in the chart.

Money, the ultimate way in which we measure value on the material plane, is associated with the power of this Center. It's easy to understand where the idea that "money is power" comes from. This translation of value on the material plane has been a growing theme on the planet for the last few hundred years.

The Will Center is connected to the Throat Center via the Channel 21/45—the Channel of Sustainable Resources. Anytime a motor connects to the Throat Center, it gives us the potential for manifesting power. The emergence of this center and channel gives us the ability to be sovereign over our own identity. This energy made it possible for us to choose who we love, what we do, follow our own path and serve our own will.

Every element in the Human Design chart is simply a potential. Type, profiles, centers, channels, and gates are just possibilities. How you choose to experience and express them is a function of choice and consciousness. As we discussed in the previous chapter, the meanings you have about who you are create your life.

As we grow and evolve, we gain more control over how we choose to utilize the potentials available to us. Awareness and consciousness expansion give us the power to consciously choose how we're going to experience and express our potential by giving us the ability to consciously influence what we attract and experience in our lives.

In the beginning, when the Will Center was a new part of our evolution, this energy gave us a drive to build, explore, conquer, and exploit the material world. The pronoun "I" became the prime directive for creating. Self-fulfillment was an aspect of this exploration.

The evolution of the Will Center gave us the energy to liberate ourselves from outdated power structures such as the church and the monarchy. It gave us the freedom to love who we choose and the ability to pursue what we desire - all big strides forward in human evolution.

As our consciousness evolved, so did our use of personal will. Our emergence into becoming a 9-centered human marked the beginning of the late modern period of history which included notable historical milestones like the French Revolution, the American Revolution, the Industrial Revolution, and the emergence of the Western World as the new leader in global wealth and power.

The Will Center is the center that is associated most commonly with material resources, usually money. In a world that is in the midst of a huge shift in consciousness, the definition of resources is changing. In Quantum Consciousness, resources not only include material resources, but energy, sustainability, community, connection, information, and relationships.

The more evolved purpose of the Will Center is to align us all with sustainability, community, truth and value. The highest expression of the Will Center is to use the "me" to serve the "we."

The misuse of our personal will and our need to evolve our definition of value, personal will and what is truly valuable is triggering cycles of disruption and upheaval. Major cycles of disruption are always a part of evolution. Whenever we hit a critical mass for growth, the old ways of living and creating become unsustainable and things fall apart as a symptom of growth and expansion.

Disruptive cycles serve to uproot us from old patterns that no longer work for our evolved consciousness. Our old meanings, stories, and identities are shattered, and we are given new opportunities to redefine who we are and engineer a new direction in life that is more in alignment with our evolved energy.

These disruptive cycles are powerful choice points that are crucial aspects of evolution. When we go through these cycles it is normal for old energies and beliefs to come into conflict with new ways of thinking and being. This conflict gives us a choice. We can either move forward and embody the new consciousness with grace and ease, or we can fight and resist our own momentum. Either way, we will evolve and change.

This is true on a personal as well as collective level. Your own inner struggles with your growth and your willingness to face the vulnerability of releasing your old identity and rewriting your personal narrative are mirrored in our collective experience. Our societies, outdated institutions, and economic structures must fall to give rise to new ways of being in community with each other.

Resistance to this process is lessened when we each do our own inner work and redefine ourselves. Our personal evolution added to the energy of the evolution of each other creates a critical mass that influences HOW we evolve. The choice to move forward peacefully rests in our hands.

As we come to the end of our current global cycle, we are facing this powerful choice point. We can either move forward and embody this new energy in an equitable, sustainable, and peaceful way or we can fight each other to end up in the same place. The big task at hand right now is to choose our path through this cycle of change.

The energies highlighted by this global cycle, the Incarnation Cross of Planning, carry the code for what we need to master during this cycle. The mastery - or not - of these energies are preparing us for the upcoming shift into the new global cycle, the Incarnation Cross of the Sleeping Phoenix.

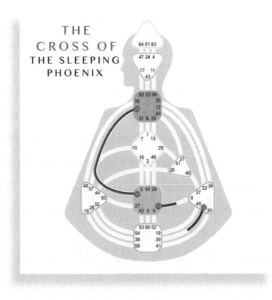

THE
CROSS OF
THE SLEEPING
PHOENIX

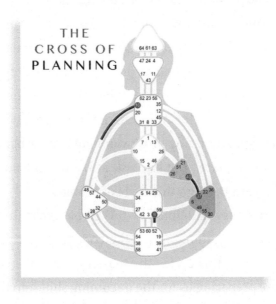

THE
CROSS OF
PLANNING

Because the Incarnation Cross of Planning focuses on the Will Center, one of the centers that emerged when we shifted from 7 to 9 centers, we see that understanding the evolving nature of the Will Center is crucial for us to cultivate more choice and influence over how we will experience our evolutionary shift.

In the beginning of our experience of will, we used this energy to codify our experiences in the material world. We used science and formulas to measure the world and to give us the confidence that we could formulate systems to create more material goods and more money.

Material gain became the measure of success, worth, and power. The more you had, the more power you had access to, and the more valuable you were. Personal gain became the goal of the will.

There is an irony in the Will Center. Even though it is often referred to as the "ego" in Human Design and, in its low expression can be very selfish, the channels connecting to the Will Center are almost exclusively from the Tribal Circuit, the circuit that has the root theme of "sharing". The only non-tribal Channel on the will is Channel 25/51, the Channel of Higher Purpose that unifies the personal self with the higher self.

The tribal configuration of the Will Center tells us that our personal self is designed to be of service to others. The wealth we create through the Will Center isn't for personal gain and to enhance our personal status. It is wealth that is designed to be shared in an equitable and sustainable way.

If you look at the configuration of the Will Center in the Cross of Planning, it is defined through Channel 37/40, The Channel of Administration. The highest expression of this channel defines the power of the Will Center as the ability to make sustainable agreements that create the peaceful administration of resources and energy.

As we come to the end of this global cycle, and we master the evolutionary challenge of the Will Center, we are now moving into an era where the value of the will is no longer how much you have, but how much you have to share.

We are redefining personal value and recognizing that we are all inherently valuable simply because we exist. There is nothing we have to do to prove our value. We are learning that every human being is an integral part of the story of humanity and, with this understanding, realizing that, to be sustainable in the world, equitability and peace are crucial to create enough for us all.

While we may not be there yet as a species, this is the evolutionary target of where we are growing. But we can't get there if we don't first deal with our own personal pain and perception of our own self-worth.

Channel 37/40 is also the energy stream that calibrates the heart, connecting the power of the Emotional Solar Plexus to the Will Center and the Identity Center (the Heart Chakra). Our emotional energy calibrates the magnetic resonance field of the heart (Magnetic Monopole) creating a state of heart coherence and influencing what experiences and manifestations we attract into our lives.

This channel and the ability to use emotional energy to consciously calibrate the heart gave us, for the first time, the ability to consciously choose and create our destiny and our life experiences. This evolutionary shift marks a giant leap in our human creative capacity and is helping us learn to create by virtue of emotional alignment rather than the use of our will. (More about that in the next chapter.)

The Will Center can only be calibrated to the level of our perception of our own value. The more valuable you perceive yourself to be, the more value you are willing to create for yourself, and the more you create for yourself, the more you have to share with others.

This is not martyrdom. The age of martyrdom is over and, by definition, not sustainable. This evolutionary shift is calling on us to heal the karma of our own self-worth so that we can use the energy of our own "enough-ness" to calibrate our hearts to create the manifestation of "enough" in the world.

It is imperative that we heal our self-worth and embrace a new definition of the value of our lives - and the value of Life. It is also vital to embody the secondary theme of the Will Center: sustainability. We are exploring how to create enough in a sustainable and enduring way.

The true power of the Will Center is not in how MUCH material wealth it has, but in its ability to sustain resources over time. The Will Center, as a motor, is designed to need cycles of rest in order to stay sustainable.

If you have a defined Will Center, you have the power to push through cycles of depletion and exhaustion with your "will power" but you can only do this for a finite period of time before you burn out. If you have an undefined Will Center, you don't have the will to push through exhaustion and, if you're not taking consistent and vital cycles of rest, you will also burn out.

Our collective conditioning has taught us that to make money you have to work and to make more money, you have to work harder. Most of us are, in some way, embodying the trauma of feeling that we are "not enough" and have trapped ourselves in a cycle of feeling that we must prove our value with our work and money. We fail to understand that we need rest, in conjunction with work, in order to be able to work and create sustainably.

We have been trained that rest is idleness and laziness, failing to properly sustain our energy and creating a cultural epidemic of burnout and exhaustion. The true power of the Will Center can't be activated without rest cycles.

In Quantum Human Design, the Will Center is called the Resource Center. It functions like an "energy bank." The more energy and resources you put in, the more you have to share.

The need to take cycles of rest and restoration is a hard thing to do when your value is tied to how much you feel you need to work to make money and when your self-worth is tied to how hard you work. If you think you don't deserve to rest because you haven't made enough money or haven't been productive enough, then you run the risk of depleting your Resource Center, further causing your value to decline. Quantum Human Design shows us that our sense of self-worth is rooted in Gate 26, the Gate of Integrity. There are five kinds of integrity associated with Gate 26. If we question our value, we may also experience a breech in any of these five areas of integrity. If we experience a breech in any of these areas of our life, it has the power to affect our self-worth.

There are five kinds of integrity:

1. **Physical Integrity** is experienced when our bodies are healthy and vital.

2. **Resource Integrity** is when we use our material resources in a sustainable way.

3. **Identity Integrity** is experienced when we feel that we can fully manifest the value of our authentic identity and we don't compromise who we are for the sake of money.

4. **Moral Integrity** is the courage to do the right thing and to make sure that your actions are

honest and aligned with high principles and values.

5. **Energetic Integrity** is experienced when we consistently and deliberately rest and take care of ourselves so that we have the energy to engage with life in a sustainable way.

We face a massive crisis in sustainability on the planet, another symptom of the imbalance of Will Center energy. Our definition of value related to resources and our failure to ensure the sustainability of our resources has us teetering on the brink of potential depletion and scarcity for everyone. Global warming presents us with a collective need to redefine how we use resources and how we can best sustain them in order to ensure the survival of all life on the planet.

We cannot create sustainable collective initiatives if we ourselves are not sustainable on a personal level. If you are struggling with your own sustainability because you are burned out and are experiencing depleted resources or if you are struggling with being in integrity, you can't make sustainable choices.

When our Will Center energy bank account is empty, our need for energy is much like a drowning person gasping for air. You are only focused on getting the next breath and not much beyond that. We must heal our own sense of value in order to be able to create beyond what is needed in the immediate moment.

When we are locked in our own inner battle for our self-worth, our need to prove our value externally keeps us from seeing the value of others. We compete for energy from others when we perceive our resources as limited instead of sustainable and abundant.

When we value ourselves enough to rest and nurture our bodies, to use our resources wisely, to be authentic with our self-expression, to do right by others, and to nurture our sustainable energy on every level, it becomes easier to see the value of every living being on the planet. We liberate ourselves from the fight for resources that we perceive are finite and limited and we move into a flow of sustainable creativity and abundant harvest.

Being sustainable means you create sustainably. Our ability to create sustainably gives us enough for ourselves as well as enough to share, the high expression of the Will Center.

Contemplations:

1. Do you love yourself? How can you deepen the expression and experience of love in your life?
2. What numbers do you use to define your value? Your weight? Your pant size? The amount of money you have

in the bank? Pay attention to how frequently we use numbers to measure our value…

3. Do you value yourself? Do you know the unique, vital and irreplaceable role you play in the cosmic plan? What do you need to do to claim and defend your value?

4. What can you do to increase your physical integrity?

5. What do you need to do to change your relationship with money?

6. What do you need to do to more fully express your authentic self in the world?

7. Do you need to realign any places where you may be out of moral integrity?

8. Do you need to set better boundaries around your energy?

9. Do you trust the Universe? Do you believe in your personal "enough-ness"? What needs to be healed for you to believe that you are enough?

Your lesson for this chapter can be found here:

CHAPTER 4

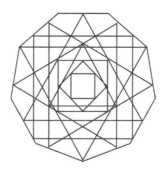

Situational Creativity versus Fundamental Creativity

Crisis and chaos are normal phases in evolutionary cycles. Periods of disruption and upheaval dismantle old infrastructures that we've "out-evolved". These cycles of disruption are simultaneously cycles of initiation, bringing in new consciousness and new aspects of the evolving human story.

We are facing an evolutionary crisis that promises to change the way in which we create. This crisis also demands of us to find solutions to the challenges facing the planet and helps us to create an equitable, sustainable, and peaceful world.

Material Consciousness and the 1781 shift in the chart solidified our ability to solve challenges using linear and formulaic thinking. Science absolutely has a place in helping us make change! But science is not the first step; it's the process we use to explore the "how" of what we are creating.

We are designed to use science and logical thinking to verify what we know. If we only look to linear, scientific formulas for the answers, we run the risk of missing the possibility of genuine change available to us.

Think about how we got to the moon. It started with a dream. Then the inspiration for the dream arrived in the form of epiphanies and "ah-ha" moments that then started the process of experimentation and exploration, which then gave us the science and the formula.

To find the solutions to the challenges facing us today, we have to consciously learn to cultivate a new kind of creative energy. Creativity must be consciously cultivated and used as a deliberate response to crisis and change.

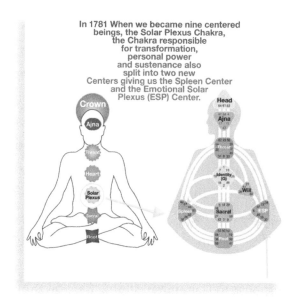

In 1781, when we became nine centered beings, the Solar Plexus Chakra, the chakra responsible for transformation, personal power, and sustenance also split into two new centers giving us the Spleen Center and the Emotional Solar Plexus Center.

The emergence of the Will Center and the new configurations of the heart of who we are, gave us a new potential to calibrate our direction with intention. This split in the Solar Plexus Chakra is giving us a different evolutionary challenge that we must master to lock in our full creative potential.

We are learning to create with emotional energy by virtue of learning how to consciously harness emotional energy and use our emotional state to calibrate our heart and the Magnetic Monopole.

We are moving away from being purely reactive, fear-motivated beings to becoming beings that can harness the power of faith as a key element of our creative power. This marks the beginning of our final delineation as human beings. We are outgrowing our purely instinctive nature.

This particular aspect of our evolution has proven to be quite challenging for us because this represents a movement away from the energy of fear as a driver for action. It's scary to not be scared and the idea of moving past fear often creates resistance and doubt, both artifacts of logical thinking!

We are not moving away from the spleen as a center but refining the way in which we use this center, learning a more evolved response to fear and mastering the power of faith as an emotional frequency to cultivate courage.

The spleen is the center for the immune system, for instinct, and for time and timing.

These three interrelated factors form the perfect trifecta for ensuring the signal for survival. The spleen gives us a gut-level feeling, often experienced as fear, that signals that something is potentially about to happen that threatens our health, life, or well-being and urges us to take action to protect ourselves.

This is a pulse that requires immediate action. It triggers an adrenaline response, raises cortisol levels, shuts down the more creative aspects of the brain, and puts us in flight or fight mode.

Obviously, if our lives are being threatened, we need to react in the moment. If a bear is chasing you, you're not going to stand around contemplating all of your potential responses or Google what to do on your phone as the bear comes barreling towards you. You're going to take relatively "thought-less" action to ensure your survival.

We have instincts, but we are not purely instinctual beings. This center is under tremendous evolutionary pressure, and it's created a deep, existential crisis for humanity. Our advanced minds, creative desires, and impulses have gotten all twisted up with our survival instincts, leaving us terrified to do things like speak on stage, write a book, or look for a new job.

We have learned to let fear drive us, to paralyze us, and to cause us to resist our natural creative impulses. So much of our personal and collective evolution and our ability to choose our future is rooted in our ability to relearn how to interpret fear and to reprogram our fear response.

Fear is not an illusion. Fear is a real response to a real-time threat to your survival. Under certain circumstances, fear is essential and healthy. It's good to be afraid of large animals, of going into a dark alley at night, or into an unlit cave. Your fear response is telling you that your life is potentially under threat and you need to be mindful and ready to react.

As we learn to draw more on the Emotional Solar Plexus as the source of our human creative potential, we are going to have to unlearn the patterns of our existential fears and to bust through these limitations that can feel so paralyzing and daunting.

The trick to busting through existential fears is learning to use the power of time and action to transcend the paralysis that fear can often trigger. Each gate of the Spleen Center has the potential to capture us in a time warp of paralyzing existential fear. When you learn to interpret these energies in a more evolved way and you embrace the understanding that these are truly places where you need to "feel the fear and do it anyway", you'll soon learn that these are time-limited fears. Actions dissipate the fear, decreases the cortisol and adrenaline response, and opens you back up to activating the human creative potential of your mind.

Any or all of the themes of the Gates of the Spleen can create conflicts in consciousness, creating a reactive response instead of a deliberate creative response.

Below is a list of the Gates of the Spleen. Explore each of the themes of these Gates and whether you've allowed yourself to get stuck in a time warp of fear with any of these themes. Remember that the only way through these fears is to take the action that is holding you back. Action breaks the hold of fear and liberates you from being trapped in a time warp of paralysis.

GATE 48

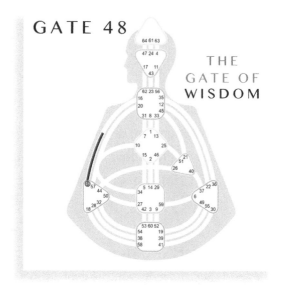

THE
GATE OF
WISDOM

Gate 48

Challenge: To allow yourself to trust that you will know what you need to know when you need to know it. To not let the fear of not knowing stop you from creating. To not let "not knowing" hold you back.

Unbalanced: Paralysis in inadequacy. To be afraid to try something new or to go beyond your comfort zone because you think you don't know or that you're not ready.

Mastery: The wisdom to explore and learn the depth of knowledge necessary to create a strong foundation for action and mastery. The self-trust to have faith in your ability to know how to know and to trust your connection to Source as the true source of your knowledge.

Contemplations: Do you trust your own knowing? What needs to be healed, released, aligned, and brought to your awareness for you to deepen your self-trust?

What practice do you have that keeps you connected to the wisdom of Source? How can you deepen your connection to Source?

Affirmation: I am a depth of wisdom and knowledge. My studies and experiences have taught me everything I need to know. I push beyond the limits of my earthly knowledge and take great leaps of faith as a function of my deep connection to Source, knowing that I will always know what I need to know when I need to know it.

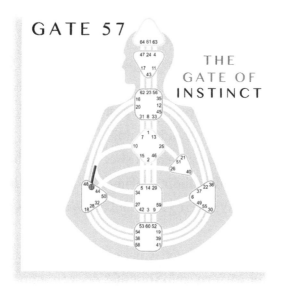

Gate 57

Challenge: To learn to trust your own insights and "gut". To learn to tell the difference between an instinctive response versus a fear of the future. To master your connection to your sense of "right" timing.

Unbalanced: To be so afraid of the future that you are paralyzed. To not trust yourself and your own instinct. To know what needs to be done to prepare for the future and to fail to act on it.

Mastery: The ability to sense when it is the right time to act. To intuitively know what needs to be made ready to be prepared for the future and to follow through on it.

Contemplations: Do you trust your intuition? What does your intuition feel like to you?

Sometimes doing a retrospective analysis of your intuition/instinct makes it clearer how your intuitive signal works. What experiences in the past have you had that you "knew" you should or shouldn't do?

How have you experienced your intuition in the past?

When you think about moving forward in your life, do you feel afraid? What are you afraid of? What can you do to mitigate the fear?

What impulses are you experiencing that are telling you to prepare for what's next in your life? Are you acting on your impulses? Why or why not?

Affirmation: My inner wisdom is deeply connected to the pulse of divine timing. I listen to my inner wisdom and follow my instinct. I know when and how to prepare the way to prepare for the future. I take guided action and I trust myself and Source.

GATE 44

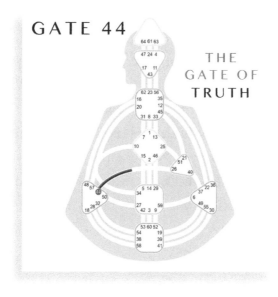

THE
GATE OF
TRUTH

Gate 44

Challenge: To not get stuck in past patterns. To cultivate the courage to go forward without being stuck in the fear of the past. To learn how to transform pain into power and to have the courage to express your authentic self without compromise or settling.

Unbalanced: Fear and paralysis that the patterns of the past are insurmountable and doomed to repeat themselves.

Mastery: The ability to see patterns that have created pain. To bring awareness to help yourself and others break old patterns and transform pain into an increased sense of value and alignment with purpose.

Contemplations: What patterns from the past are holding you back from moving forward with courage?

Do you see how your experiences from the past have helped you learn more about who you truly are? What have you learned about your value and your power?

What needs to be healed, released, aligned, and brought to your awareness for you to fully activate your power?

What needs to be healed, released, aligned, and brought to your awareness for you to step boldly into your aligned and authentic path?

Affirmation:

I am powerfully intuitive and can sense the patterns that keep others stuck in limiting beliefs and constricted action. Through my insights and awareness, I help others break free from past limiting patterns and learn to find the power in their pain, find the blessings in their challenges and help them align more deeply with an authentic awareness of their true value and purpose.

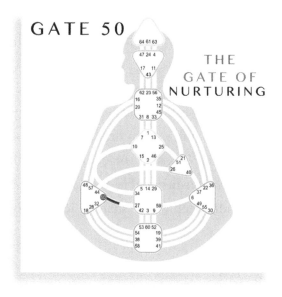

GATE 50

THE GATE OF NURTURING

Gate 50

Challenge: To transcend guilt and unhealthy obligation and do what you need to do to take care of yourself in order to better serve others. To hold to rigid principles that keep you from responding to what others need. To judge others based on limiting values that disallow for compassion.

Unbalanced: To over-care. To let guilt stop you from sustaining yourself. To hold to rigid principles and to struggle to allow others the consequences of their choices.

Mastery: The ability to nurture yourself so that you have more to give others. The intuition to know what others need to bring them into greater alignment with Love. To teach and share what you have to increase the wellbeing of others.

Contemplations: How do you feel about taking care of yourself first? How do you sustain your nurturing energy?

What role does guilt play in driving and/or motivating you? What would you choose if you could remove the guilt?

Do you have non-negotiable values? What are they? How do you handle people who share different values from you?

Affirmation:

My presence brings love into the room. I nurture and love others. I take care of myself first in order to be better able to serve Love. I intuit what people need, and I facilitate for them a state of self-love and self-empowerment by helping them align more deeply with the power of Love. I let go and I allow others to learn from what I model and teach. I am a deep well of love that sustains the planet.

GATE 32

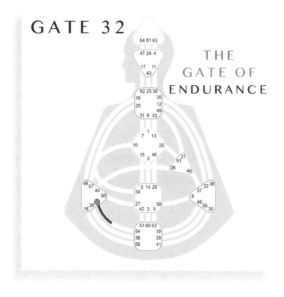

THE
GATE OF
ENDURANCE

Gate 32

Challenge: To trust in divine timing. To prepare for the next step of manifestation and to align with the unfolding of the process. To be patient.

Unbalanced: Letting the fear of failure cause you to avoid preparing what you need to do. To not be ready when the timing is right. To push too hard, too fast, too long against right timing.

Mastery: The awareness of what needs to be done to make a dream a manifested reality. Setting the stage, preparation, being ready. The patience to trust that once the stage is set, the timing will unfold as needed to serve the highest good of all. To translate divine inspiration into readiness.

Contemplations: What do you need to do to be prepared to manifest your vision? What actionable steps need to be completed in order for you to be ready when the timing is right?

What do you need to do to cultivate patience?

Do you have a fear of failing that is causing you to avoid being prepared?

Are you over-doing and being overly prepared? Are you pushing too hard? What can you let go of?

Affirmation:

I am a divine translator for divine inspiration. I sense and know what needs to be prepared on the earthly plane in order to be ready for right timing. I am aligned with right timing, and I prepare and wait patiently, knowing that when the time is right, I will be ready to do the work to help transform pain into power.

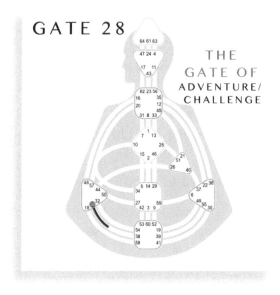

GATE 28

THE
GATE OF
ADVENTURE/
CHALLENGE

Gate 28

Challenge: To not let struggle and challenge leave you feeling defeated and despairing. To learn to face life as an adventure. Do not let challenge and struggle cause you to feel as if you've failed.

Unbalanced: Refusing to take action out of fear that the journey will be too painful, wrought with struggle, or that you will fail. To feel like a failure. To fall into victim consciousness.

Mastery: To learn to share from your personal experience, your struggles, and your triumphs. To persevere and to know that the adventures in your life deepen your ability to transform life into a meaningful journey. To understand that your struggles help deepen the collective ideas about what is truly valuable and worthy of creating.

Contemplations: How can you turn your challenge into adventure? Where do you need to cultivate a sense of adventure in your life?

What do you need to do to rewrite the story of your "failures?"

What meanings, blessings, and lessons have you learned from your challenges?

What needs to be healed, released, aligned, and brought to your awareness for you to trust yourself and your choices?

What do you need to do to forgive yourself for your perceived past failures?

Affirmation:

I am here to push the boundaries of life and what is possible. I thrive in situations that challenge me. I am an explorer on the leading edge of consciousness and my job is to test how far I can go. I embrace challenge. I am an adventurer. I share all that I have learned from my challenges with the world. My stories help give people greater meaning, teach them what is truly worthy of creating, and inspire people to transform.

GATE 18

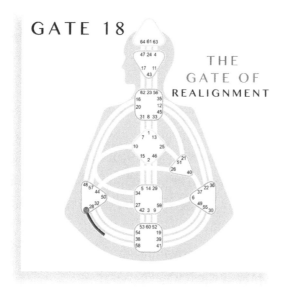

THE
GATE OF
REALIGNMENT

Gate 18

Challenge: To learn to wait for the right timing and the right circumstances to offer your intuitive insights into how to fix or correct a pattern. To wait for the right time and the right reason to share your critique. To understand that the purpose of re-alignment is to create more joy, not to be "right".

Unbalanced: To be critical. To share criticism without respect for the impact. To be more concerned with your own "rightness" rather than assess whether your insight is actually adding to more joy in the world.

Mastery: To see a pattern that needs correcting and to wait for the right timing and circumstances to correct and align it. To serve joy.

Contemplations: What does joy mean to you? How do you serve it?

How do you cultivate joy in your own life?

How does it feel to be "right" about something and keep it to yourself? Do you need to release any old "stories" about needing to be "right?"

Do you trust your own insights? Do you have the courage to share them when it's necessary?

Affirmation:

I am a powerful force that re-aligns patterns. My insights and awareness gives people the information they need to deepen their mastery and to experience greater joy. I serve joy and I align the patterns of the world to increase the world's potential for living in the flow of joy.

Our biology wants us to react to crisis situations. Our adrenaline "fight or flight" reaction kicks in. The expansive creative response that is an innate aspect of our human potential shuts down in favor of more vital and limited splenic survival-based reactions.

This level of primal reactivity is called situational creativity. Situational creativity happens in the moment. It's reactive, determined by your conditioning, and offers short-term solutions.

Situational creativity is finite. It offers solutions that come from the conditioned mind and is the result of "thinking" or figuring things out. If you know Human Design, you know that for most of us, our "thinking" is a deeply conditioned way of processing information and is often either pressurized or somewhat flawed.

Situational creativity can be destructive. It's a response to systems that instill fear and the need to fight for survival in us. Destruction is an important part of the creative process. We need to move things out of the way in order to create space for something new.

But once we are standing in the space that we have created, we have to slow down the reactive process and harness the full potential of our creative power. We have to consciously harness our fundamental creativity.

Fundamental creativity transcends our conditioning. It moves us out of a reactive, adrenalized state into a flow of pure creative response. It transcends our conditioning and past behavioral patterns. We experience fundamental creativity in the form of an "a-ha" moment or an epiphany.

These epiphanies often happen when we are "distracted" and doing something enjoyable like taking a relaxing shower, going for a walk, or playing with paints and glitter. We aren't actually distracted during these activities, but because we are relaxed, our cortisol levels are decreased and our dopamine and serotonin levels are elevated, causing the brain to be more available for expansive solutions to the challenges facing us.

SITUATIONAL CREATIVITY	FUNDAMENTAL CREATIVITY
In the monent	Transcends Conditioning
Reactive	Epiphany "Ah - Ha"
Determined by your conditioning	Infinite Source (Realm of Archetypes and beyond...)
Short term solution	Imaginative and possibility oriented
Finite - Comes from the confitioned mind	Aligns with cosmic order
The result of "thinking" and reasoning (The Mind)	Un- "reasonable"
Reasonable	Deliberate

We won't find the solutions to the challenges ahead of us if we're stressed, burned out, overwhelmed, or in a state of panic. To cultivate a higher state of fundamental creativity, we have to nurture ourselves, rest, restore, and replenish our connection to Source and keep ourselves in a conscious state of relaxation and joy.

Fundamental creativity comes from Infinite Source (the Quantum Field) and offers us solutions that often interrupt the patterns of what has come before. It is "out of the box" thinking that challenges us to take a leap of faith and try something new. Fundamental creativity is imaginative and possibility oriented, aligns with the bigger cosmic plan and is inherently "unreasonable", meaning it defies the patterns of what has come before.

The Emotional Solar Plexus, the second center created from the split of the Solar Plexus Chakra, gave us the power to use emotional frequencies as a source of our creative power. The emergence of the Emotional Solar Plexus sets up the energetic hard wiring for us to be able to consciously use emotional energy to calibrate the Magnetic Monopole and to become more fundamentally creative and deliberate instead of situationally creative and reactive.

This center, like the spleen, is also under a tremendous amount of evolutionary pressure. Emotional energy and how we interpret and use it is changing. We have to first define what emotions are NOT in order to realize what emotional energy actually IS.

When I worked as a parent educator in my twenties, I spent a lot of my parenting classes teaching parents the vocabulary of "feelings". I used a lot of charts and worksheets to help parents give themselves and their children language to describe their emotional state.

Parents learned to start emotional conversations with the phrase, "I feel_____." I specifically used this phrase because we often talk about emotions with sentences that start with, "I am_____." I am angry. I am frustrated. I am sad.

You can't "be" an emotion. Emotions are dynamic, not static. You can feel them in the moment and use your emotional awareness to let you know how close or far you are from being in alignment with what you want or with how much you desire to be in the situation you are experiencing.

The minute you start to identify with your emotions, is the minute you lock yourself into them and hold on to them, creating a myriad of challenges for yourself. You also lose your ability to use this incredibly powerful source of energy to deliberately program your experience of reality.

The first thing you can do to activate the true nature of your creativity is to start speaking about your emotions in terms of how you feel or how you are experiencing emotional energy in the moment. Using phrases such as, "I am feeling _____" or "I am experiencing the feeling of _____" allows you to explore your emotional alignment in the moment instead of holding on to an emotional state that dampens your awareness and creative capacity.

The Emotional Solar Plexus is a motor in Human Design. The energy of the Emotional Solar Plexus fluctuates in waves.

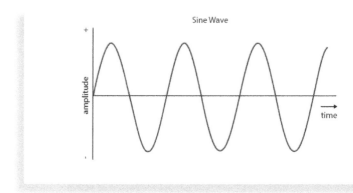

The current nature of our emotional energy is volatile and changeable. You are going to have fluctuations in your emotional energy as you learn to consciously harness this energy to calibrate your Magnetic Monopole and create in a flow state.

If you look at the wave pattern of emotional energy and you drew a line across the midpoint of the peaks and valleys of the sine wave, you'd define the baseline frequency of your emotional state. This baseline frequency is, in essence, the frequency that defines your prayer field, the energy that is calibrating your Magnetic Monopole and setting the direction for your life.

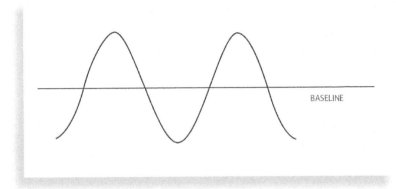

Our sense of timing changes with the Emotional Solar Plexus. The Spleen Center and instinct demand our attention immediately. There is tremendous potential for pressure to do and create in the moment, which is vital if you're reacting to a life-threatening situation, but not so good for our more human creative endeavors.

Creating takes time. It takes practice. It takes mastery. It requires us to filter through all of the factors in the creative equation to make sure that what we are intending is not only good for us, but also sustainable and good for the world.

Think about it. If we manifested instantly all the things we are thinking when we drive on the highway in rush hour, it probably wouldn't be very pretty or good for the world.

The Emotional Solar Plexus demands alignment and a frequency of energy that is held and sustained. Our thinking, imaginations, contemplations, and our willingness to engage in mental explorations of possibilities create emotional energy. This emotional energy gives us the experience of being in a flow state. It programs us to look for synchronicities and aligned evidence that keeps us moving along the path that is the unfolding of the manifestation of our emotional energy.

In other words, your emotional energy creates not only what you are consciously intending to create, but a reality that matches the quality of the thoughts and emotions you are generating.

There is forgiveness in the Emotional Solar Plexus in the way that it functions at this time on the planet. We create from our baseline frequency over time, not from the moment-to-moment fluctuations in our emotional state.

That means you can have "bad" days or "bad" thoughts and not uncreate what you're creating. You must simply learn to keep shifting your thinking and feeling as close to your baseline frequency as possible.

In the original predictions from Ra Uru Hu about the Solar Plexus Mutation, he noted that the wave-like function of the Emotional Solar Plexus would stabilize and become more fixed in place. This is not a mechanical change but rather a change that happens as we consciously learn to cultivate emotional energy as our creative power.

At this stage of our evolution, we are still untangling ourselves from our karmic patterns. We are unbinding ourselves from thought forms that created infrastructures that institutionalized divisive consciousness and the fear of lack. As we move through the final stages of disentanglement and into the next phase of evolution of the Human Design body graph and our energy blueprint, we will speed up our creative process and the emotional fluctuations of the Emotional Solar Plexus will stabilize. We will no longer have to take into account our ancestral conditioning as an influencer of the creative process. It will become easier and easier to hold to your baseline frequency.

Our energy field and our Human Design charts are the manifestations of our consciousness. Human Design is the mechanics of the human experience, but each chart needs a driver to run the chart. Changing the hard wiring of the human story is like upgrading to a nicer car. No matter how different your experience of the car is, you still have to decide how you're going to drive it, the quality of the road you're going to travel on and the kind of journey you're going to take.

Consciousness determines the quality of the journey of your life. The evolved change in the hard wiring of the chart supports stabilizing the volatility of the emotional wave, increasing the probability of peace on the planet, but we have to use conscious intention to stabilize the emotional wave.

Your focused energy and intention create an elevation in the baseline frequency of the emotional wave. This shift in frequency diminishes the amount of time spent in either a high state or a low state. Your perception of changes in your emotional state is minimized, increasing your ability to continue to harness the power of deliberate management of this powerful creative energy.

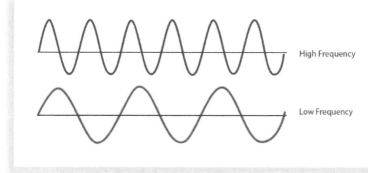

The emergence of the Emotional Solar Plexus, the Will Center, and the circuitry that connects the Emotional Solar Plexus, the Will and the Identity Center also gave us the hard wiring to consciously calibrate the Magnetic Monopole. We now have the ability to, with intention and attention, stabilize the emotional wave and create a frequency of emotional energy that calibrates the Magnetic Monopole to attract experiences into your life that match the frequency and quality of your emotional energy.

We are moving from "feelings" being a way in which we define our reaction to our lives, to using emotional energy as a way of consciously programming a prayer field that influences what we create in our lives.

Remember that evolution doesn't happen in a flash. It takes time. For the last two hundred years we've been preparing for this change. As we near the conclusion of the Cross of Planning and move into the Cross of the Sleeping Phoenix, we are mastering our ability to use emotional energy to consciously and deliberately create.

This skillset gives us the power to focus our intention and align it with our "upgraded" hard wiring, to stabilize the emotional volatility of the human condition, and clears the path for us to fulfill the potential of consciously and deliberately creating a world of equitable, sustainable peace.

Your lesson for this chapter can be found here:

CHAPTER 5

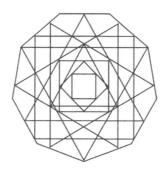

*From the Cross of Planning
to the Cross of the Sleeping
Phoenix: A Test of Time,
Faith, and Alignment*

The planets bring us the information stream of our evolutionary program. The energy of the planets is expressed through the 64 gates in Human Design. Each planet brings its own theme of growth and highlights it through the various gates on the Human Design mandala. The planets, in essence, bring the themes of our soul curriculum. What we are learning as humans on earth helps consciousness evolve.

Each planet moves at its own speed with its own influence. Each rotation of the planet measures a cycle of expansion, with its own theme. The earth itself has its own cycle of expansion measured on an annual basis where it travels around the sun in a calendar year.

The earth has a second cycle that is much bigger that measures the gradual shift in the orientation of the earth's axis of rotation. This rotation completes a cycle approximately every 25,772 years. We call this cycle the Precession of the Equinoxes.

Within this major earth cycle are six epochs broken into eight smaller cycles. The smaller cycles within the epochs last approximately 400 years. These global cycles bring the bigger themes for the evolution of humanity. They are, in essence, the plot outline in the story of our growth and expansion. Each global cycle is expressed through specific Human Design gates.

As the planet evolves, it goes through global cycles. Global cycles set the stage for our evolutionary "story". It is the background themes that humanity must master as part of our evolution.

Our current global cycle began in 1615 and carries the energy of the Cross of Planning through Gates 37, 40, 9, and 16.

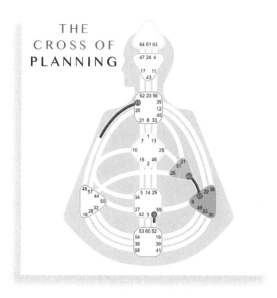

THE CROSS OF PLANNING

The "plot outline" of our evolutionary story for the last 400 years is illuminated in the Cross of Planning. The configuration of this cross gives us big clues into what we need to complete and master both personally and collectively in order to be prepared for the next cycle of our growth.

The first theme that the Cross of Planning holds for us is rooted in Channel 40/37, the Channel of Administration. The mastery of this channel gives us the ability to make sustainable agreements that create the peaceful administration of resources and energy.

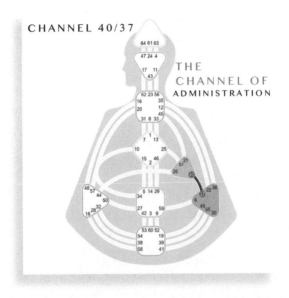

CHANNEL 40/37

There are several key concepts that we have been exploring both personally and collectively in this channel. This channel contains the potential for sustainable peace and peaceful agreements but only if we are aligning with the energy of "enough."

Channel 40/37 emerged during the mutation in 1781 and gave us the new ability to be able to consciously calibrate the heart with our emotional energy and consequently influence the Magnetic Monopole and what we attract into our lives.

The more we feel that we are "enough," that we have "enough," and that there is enough to share, the more our heart is calibrated with that frequency of energy and the more we attract "enough" into our lives.

The Will Center is the center that translates value on the material plane. At this stage in our evolution we translate value into money, material resources, and wealth. This center is under tremendous evolutionary pressure as we reach the end of this global cycle, setting us up for the themes of the Solar Plexus Mutation in 2027 and the energy of the Cross of the Sleeping Phoenix.

In the final thrust of the Cross of Planning, we are redefining what is valuable and what we value. With a planet facing a crisis in sustainability and resources, we are learning that value is not measured in things but in quality of life. Global warming and other challenges facing the planet are potentially great equalizing events. We all live under the same sun and breathe the same air and it serves us all to ensure that our planet survives and is sustainable.

What good are material resources if the planet itself is dying?

Remember here, as we discuss this, that what we are experiencing on the planet is the result of the evolution of our consciousness. While it may feel that we've "screwed up" and created a crisis, on a collective consciousness level, we created this as an opportunity to seed the next level of our evolution. These critical challenges are forcing us to have to discover new ways of creating and collaborating that will shift our perspective and give us the potential to redefine the old paradigms of the past and embody a new level of conscious creativity.

As material consciousness dies off and we integrate quantum consciousness into our personal and collective realities, we stop using material metrics - numbers - to measure value. Our value will no longer be determined by the size of our bank account, the quantity of "stuff" we own, or even how many years of education we have.

Quantum consciousness informs us that every sentient being has a unique, vital, and irreplaceable role in the cosmic plan and we are all inherently valuable because we exist. There is nothing we have to do to "earn" our value. Our new evolutionary challenge is to set up a world that embodies this ideal. Imagine a world where we all value the unique role that each of us plays in the collective story of who we all are!

The theme of sustainability also lives in Channel 40/37. For the Will Center to operate optimally and for it to have sustainable energy it needs cycles of rest. The "enough-ness" of the Will Center is determined by how much energy it has access to.

The energy of the Will Center is like a bank account. When it has energy in the bank, it has the will power to regulate itself, temper its emotional response, and to act deliberately honoring the agreements that it makes and sharing sustainably. A resourced Will Center has the energy to claim and defend true value and stays aligned with the actions necessary to embody value.

This is true both personally and collectively. If we do not value ourselves enough to keep our energy bank full, we become depleted and burned out. We project onto others that they should be filling our energy bank for us and we become angry and hurt that people aren't taking care of us when, in actuality, we need to be taking care of ourselves.

Being depleted also decreases our creative response. When we are burned out and tired, we become stressed because our energy reserves are low, and we are scared that we won't have enough energy to do what we need to do to sustain ourselves. This stress causes cortisol levels to rise, decreasing dopamine and serotonin making us more situationally creative and reactive. This creates a domino effect that makes it harder to sustain peaceful agreements and to take sustainable action.

We create the energy that we embody. If we are burned out and unsustainable with our energy, it is difficult for us to create sustainably in the world. We can't craft sustainable agreements. We don't use our resources sustainably. We can't sustain peace and we, ultimately, blame others for not doing for us what we need to be doing for ourselves.

This is the challenge that this channel brings us during this era. Can we shift our definition of value, learn to create sustainable and consequently set up enduring, peaceful agreements that create a flow of sustainable resources for us all?

The flow of energy through Channel 40/37 to the Will Center gives us the ability to consciously use emotional energy to calibrate the heart. All of the energies in the chart have the potential, based on the meanings we assign them from our own conditioning, to be expressed as a "high" or "low" expression.

The gates of Channel 40/37 give us the code to maximizing the highest potential expression of the human condition. We have the ability to influence the evolution of the world through our ability to consciously harness our emotional energy. The gates in Channel 40/37 tell us the themes we must cultivate to express the highest potential of our human condition.

Gate 37, the Gate of Harmony, is located on the Emotional Solar Plexus informing us of the energy necessary to create sustainability and to shift our value paradigm. The Gate of Harmony teaches us that we have to first cultivate inner peace in order to master the emotional alignment to make peaceful and sustainable choices no matter what's going on in the outer world.

Gate 40, the Gate of Restoration, shows us that in order to have resources to share in a sustainable way, we must learn to value ourselves enough to retreat from community and the energy of those we love to restore, restock, and replenish our inner resources.

This gate helps us to move out of martyrdom and into the understanding that if we have high self-worth, we know we are valuable enough to take responsibility for our own care and resources. This is a vital energy that facilitates peaceful agreements and contracts. If we fail to re-source ourselves, we often abdicate our own power to take care of ourselves, creating resentment, hurt and even anger in response to "not feeling taken care of."

This is a crucial component to establishing a world rooted in equitable, sustainable peace. When people feel that they ARE enough, nurture their energy and their resources, recognize value can only be self-generated, and take responsibility for the quality of peace and sustainability they generate from healing their own self-worth karma, then they enter into healthy, sustainable, and peaceful agreements.

Healing the karma of any event, circumstance, or experience that has caused you to doubt your lovability, self-worth, or lose your connection to your right place in the world, is the most important thing we need to do to prepare ourselves for the next global cycle.

The second two gates in the Cross of Planning are Gate 9, the Gate of Convergence, and Gate 16, the Gate of Zest. Both of these energies together give us the focused enthusiasm to overcome obstacles and to master sustaining the emotional alignment needed to create the necessary shifts to evolve towards peace.

Gate 9 teaches us that when we can focus on the end goal and the big picture of what we want and where we are headed, the next right step to creating peace manifests before us. We don't have to figure out what to do or what action to take. We simply need to stay focused and hold our prayer field and the outer manifestation of our reality will reveal what work needs to be done and what action steps need to be taken.

Gate 16 gives us the courage to leap into action and to inspire others to act, even if we don't know all the details. This is the courage to trust your own intuition that the timing is right and that you are ready enough - even if you don't know exactly how your journey will unfold. The zest of Gate 16 helps you have faith in the outcome even if you don't know how the path in front of you will unfold.

Altogether, the Cross of Planning has helped us learn that when we create from the energy of high self-worth and we embody the energy of our "enough-ness," we create enough. We create sustainably and we enter into peaceful and enduring agreements that facilitate the creation of even more value and well-being that increases the quality of life for everyone. We learn that focus and enthusiasm are key components to cultivating the faith that when we rest versus overwork, when we cultivate our inner sense of value instead of allowing external metrics to measure our worth, we are safe and sustained.

This global cycle has taught us to keep our focus on creating a prayer field before us, to zestfully tend to our emotional alignment with peace and to heal our personal karma around our self-worth as a way of shifting our collective paradigm. This gives us the understanding that value is not a zero-sum game. It's an infinite, ever-expanding state. Knowing our own value supports us in being able to fully see the value of others without a hidden agenda, making the possibility for equitable, sustainable peace viable.

In the year 2027, we move into a new global cycle that carries the energy of the Cross of the Sleeping Phoenix through Gates 55, 34, 20, and 59.

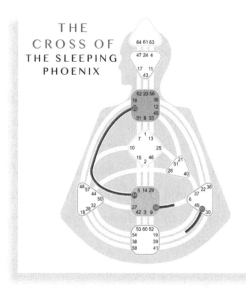

Before I share more information with you about this upcoming global cycle, I want to revisit some ideas about planetary transits and global cycles in particular. Planetary transits bring us themes. I am concerned that sometimes when we talk about transitory themes, we forget that we are still in integrity with our human nature.

If we simply focus on the theme and think we are becoming the theme, we are forgetting who we truly are. If the Human Design chart is a blueprint for the human story, we only have to look at the Identity Center and the Will Center (formerly the Heart Chakra) to know that we are loving beings.

We are designed to love ourselves first as the foundation of our ability to share and to love others. We are designed to have a sovereign voice over our own leadership. We are created to fulfill the full expression of who we are and each and every life we live is a canvas for the expression of the Divine in human form.

We are given the ability to define our direction from our personal narrative. We have the power to change our personal narrative if we want to change the direction of our lives.

We are designed to work in partnership with Source and our unique, vital, and irreplaceable role in the cosmic plan gives us the ability to co-create. We are not victims of some capricious program.

We are designed to be physically vital and to love ourselves enough to fully embody our bodies. We are designed to love our bodies and to fully enjoy the sensual experience of being alive and testing the limits of being spirits in human form.

We are designed to receive all the support and sufficiency we need to completely fulfill our story. Learning to allow ourselves to be supported is one of the lessons we learn with the shift in definition of value in the Will Center. You are designed to be supported because you are a once-in-a-lifetime cosmic event and you are worthy of support.

We are designed to, once we have tapped into our own "enough-ness," to share what we have with others from a place of compassion and without hidden agendas. We share because it feels good, not because we're trying to prove that we are good.

You. Are. Good.

We are designed to use our lives to serve the unfolding of the evolution of humanity and each other. We are designed to regulate ourselves so that we can sustain ourselves and be more, have more, and give more. We are designed to care for each other and to make peaceful agreements that allow others to be more, have more, and give more. We are beautifully crafted to live in integrity with who we truly are, our authentic selves. This state of authentic alignment keeps us healthy and thriving and fully embodied in the earth story.

This is who we are and no matter how the chart shifts and changes or whatever planetary weather may be illuminating the skies, this part of our story doesn't change. I believe that the transits seek to support us in expanding upon who we are, not altering the basic nature of the human story.

We are evolving so that we can more fully experience the adventure of living as spiritual beings in human stories. We are learning to expand our creative potential in phenomenal ways. I believe that the entire cosmos is watching us and cheering us on!

We are moving into a new 400-year Global Cycle that brings us the learning themes rooted in the Incarnation

Cross of the Sleeping Phoenix. Let's begin our exploration of this Cross by looking first at the overall theme of this Cross.

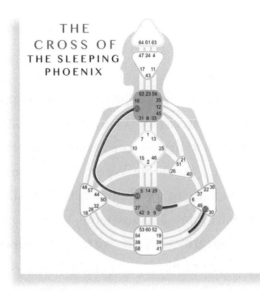

THE
CROSS OF
THE SLEEPING
PHOENIX

There is a small challenge with completely fleshing out exactly what the energy of this cross will mean for us over the next 400 years. Remember that the Cross of Planning contained the Will Center, the Solar Plexus, and Channel 40/37, all aspects of the chart that only appeared during the shift of 1781, midway through this global cycle.

We can make an educated guess as to what this cross means for us, but the hard wiring of the gates and channels in the Cross of the Sleeping Phoenix are all parts of circuitry that is about to change with the 2027 mutation, bringing us a new way of expanding the human story.

Think about this. Before the emergence of the Will Center and the ability to consciously calibrate the Magnetic Monopole, it was a very new concept to be able to engineer your own destiny. People didn't have the consciousness and the hard wiring to be able to really comprehend this idea at the beginning of our current global cycle.

As we enter a new global cycle, it is difficult for us to be able to imagine exactly where we are headed and how our world will transform in response. The one thing that stays constant is the heart of who we are. The Identity Center and the Will Center will be calibrated by equitability, sustainability, and the potential for sufficient, sustainable resources to enhance the possibility of peace. Our evolution up until this point clearly points the way to an expression of humanity that is unified, compassionate, creative, and constructs a world that reflects this expression.

Just like the mythical phoenix bird, the Cross of the Sleeping Phoenix has the potential, through cycles of rebirth and transformation to return to a life in paradise. Certainly, the potential for paradise lies in the future of our world.

The gates and channels in the Cross of the Sleeping Phoenix tell a story of the potential for transformative, responsive leadership and empowerment that can unify and provide sustainable resources for all when we create with faith and emotional alignment. We may not know how we're going to get what we need, but if we trust and keep ourselves emotionally aligned, the next right step will manifest and all we have to do is respond to what shows up.

Channel 34/20, the Channel of Responsive Power (the Channel of Power and Charisma) defines both the Throat Center and the Sacral Center in this Cross. The nature of how this Channel functions will change as the chart changes in 2027. Currently, this is part of a circuit called the Unifying Circuit (Integration Circuit).

This channel defines the archetype of the Manifesting Generator. It is the only channel that connects the Sacral Center directly to the Throat Center without passing through any other Centers. It is the most powerful Channel in the Human Design chart, giving us the theme of sustainable responsive energy that is expressed in response to what's needed.

The mastery of the theme of this channel teaches us to trust that when our response and power is required, the opportunity to take the lead will show itself. To fully activate and utilize this incredible power to "do", we have to manage our energy so that it stays sustainable.

This next cycle tasks us with learning to trust in the timing of the universe. We are mastering waiting patiently and preparing to take action when the timing is right and to keep our energy occupied while we wait. We are activating a level of personal empowerment and letting go of playing small.

As the chart changes, a new circuit—the Binary Circuit—emerges. In the Binary Circuit, Channel 34/20 gains its direction from the Identity Center through Gate 10, the

Gate of Self-Love, and from Channel 25/51, the Channel of Higher Purpose.

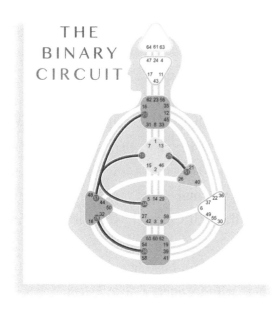

THE BINARY CIRCUIT

Channel 34/20 in this new configuration gains its power from responding to the needs of others through the Sacral Center and it takes its direction from living from aligning with higher purpose and heart. In other words, one of our major learning themes in the next global cycle is to master unifying ourselves around common spiritual principles that bring us together to respond to the needs of humanity.

In the current configuration of Channel 34/20, it is easy to see how one interpretation of the new era we are entering might be that we are all hunkered down in bunkers following our own direction. Certainly, even in the new configuration of the Binary Circuit people could be "self-ish." Self-love and alignment with your right place in the cosmic plan—your Higher Purpose—is indeed selfish but it's that level of selfishness that inevitably defaults to being in service to the expression of love in the world. This is the higher potential of this expression of 34/20, the ability to sustainably and responsively put love into action and, ultimately, a shift into a more feminine style of leadership that is aligning and caring.

Gate 59, the Gate of Sustainability, is a part of Tribal Circuitry, circuitry in the chart that is driven by the theme of caring for others. The flow of this energy in the Cross of the Sleeping Phoenix makes it to the Throat Center, the Center for Action, through Channel 34/20, giving it even more power.

This gate is an aura-busting energy that penetrates the auras of others with its energy. Gate 59 cares that everyone has food and resources and is willing to do the "work" necessary to provide and share. This Gate challenges us with learning to make abundant choices that sustain us individually and, at the same time, sustain others. We will learn to better collaborate and initiate others into sustainable relationships from a place of sufficiency and to learn to share what we have in a sustainable way.

The last gate in the Cross of the Sleeping Phoenix, Gate 55, the Gate of Faith, signifies the final shift in our innate creative capacity. To fully unpack this power of this shift, we have to look at all of the aspects of this gate.

The lesson of Gate 55 is to master the ability to hold the emotional frequency of energy and the vision for a creation and to trust in sufficiency so deeply that you're able to create without limitation. In other words, when we can hold on to an emotional frequency that matches what we want to be experiencing in our lives, we are essentially creating an energetic prayer field that pulls life experiences into our lives that match our frequency of energy. Our faith ensures that we do not entertain the fear of lack. This empowers us to take seemingly impossible leaps of faith with our creativity and gives us the ability to create the solutions to the challenges facing humanity today and beyond.

Physically, this gate is associated with the pancreas, digestion, and assimilation. This signifies the ultimate relationship between Source, food, and sufficiency. When we hold the energy of faith, we are supported and nurtured on every level. Our connection to Source is the sweetness of life and is the ultimate definition of abundance.

We are redefining abundance, which is a term I'm hesitant to use because I believe our current definition of abundance is rooted in overcompensating for our lack of our own perception of "enough-ness." Our need to prove our "enoughness" has caused us to overuse resources in a dishonoring and unbalanced way.

We see with Gate 55, the relationship between food and Source. We can enhance our ability to hold higher frequencies of energy by changing the way we eat. Unprocessed, whole foods that are fresh from the ground enhance our energy and support our bodies in holding higher frequencies of energy. As you will see in the next chapter when we look at the new changes in the body graph, our relationship with food is shifting dramatically.

When we are holding higher frequencies of energy, we begin to sustain a state of higher alertness and positive expectation. We program our hearts and minds to see the opportunities that match the frequency of energy that we are holding.

Energy medicine practitioners such as homeopaths have always known that higher frequencies of energy can penetrate lower frequencies and elevate them. When we learn to hold higher frequencies of energy, we are better able to lift the energy of others. Both Gate 34 and Gate 59 are already aura-busting energies. Adding the elevated frequency of faith to the mix informs us that we are able to lift others up with our own energy during this time of transition. Now, more than ever, it is vital that we consciously cultivate an energy of faith to support and enhance the experience of, not only ourselves, but also the people surrounding us.

(Did you know that having a happy neighbor increases your chances of being happy, a higher frequency of energy, by 60 percent?)

When we hold the frequency of faith, we calibrate the Magnetic Monopole to attract into our experience, the things we need to fulfill our faith. Without the fear of lack, we can freely transcend our previous limitations and fear, expanding our creative capacity exponentially. We are able to attract the seemingly impossible by virtue of holding a frequency of energy that aligns with new possibilities from the Quantum Field. We solidly move from being situationally creative to living in a constant state of fundamental creativity.

This gives us the ability to stay in a constant state of resilience. We consciously harness the outflow of high-frequency energy and we can sustain this state no matter what is going on around us, ultimately influencing the outcome of what we are experiencing in the world.

Just as the Cross of Service initiated the Scientific Revolution and the emergence of material consciousness, the Cross of the Sleeping Phoenix marks the beginning of a powerful creative revolution and finalizes the advancement from material consciousness to quantum consciousness.

Your lesson for this chapter can be found here:

CHAPTER 6

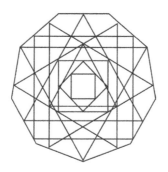

The Mechanics
of the Shift

In this next section you're going to learn about the mechanical changes happening in the Human Design chart. It is difficult to really understand from our current human perspective exactly how these changes may feel to us as our world transforms. These are new energies, new manifestations of consciousness, and we may not have the paradigm, at this stage of our development, to completely understand them.

Really feel the words as you read this section. The story of the changes in the chart has been traditionally told in a different way than I'm sharing this with you. We are deeply conditioned with post-apocalyptic fantasies and dystopian perspectives.

What if the story of the evolution of consciousness through the experience of human life has a beautiful and happy ending? What if our conditioning is keeping us from seeing this truth?

You get to decide what is truth to you. If it feels correct, then it's your truth. This is the true gift of knowing your Human Design. You get to decide what resonates for you.

The mechanical changes in the chart won't necessarily happen all at once. This shift will occur in waves and has already been in us on a genetic level for a while. This section offers a breakdown of how the chart is changing and some guesses as to how these changes may manifest on the planet.

The outer world is the outward manifestation of consciousness. We have a tendency to think that our outer world is something different than our consciousness and inner terrain of our hearts and mind. There is an interplay between the inner and outer, external events impacting our inner experience of consciousness and internal alignment affecting our outer experience.

As the evolution progresses, we will see changes that will be easy to interpret as something "out there" that is happening to us. It is all us. Even terrible events, such as a pandemic, are aspects of our collective consciousness. It's crucial to not interpret this linearly or with blame, but rather to see that some of the evolution of humanity will seemingly happen externally first and that consciousness creates opportunities in many interesting and often unpredictable ways.

We may tend to interpret these events as a collective coincidence, but as the big picture continues to unfold, we will see that many events that occur on the outer plane will turn out to be seminal experiences that change all of humanity. The spiritual evolution of humanity will ultimately impact the mundane.

I say this because so many times we expect phenomenal spiritual signs and wonders to gauge the progress of our spiritual growth. Those of us who are enamored with more dramatic spiritual stories can often miss the "sign" of real spiritual evolution. We wait for the flaming apparition of an archangel or a spirit guide at the foot of our bed in the middle of the night to give us a sign" Sometimes the sign is a change in a Supreme Court ruling or a collective move towards plant-based eating.

It's pleasantly surprising to me that many of the changes that I intuited 15 years ago, when I first started teaching this information, are already happening in the world. I fully expect for more of these changes to manifest over the course of my life.

In this next section, I will outline the stages of the Solar Plexus Mutation and the changes we are seeing in the Human Design chart. I will share with you potential manifestations of these changes with the awareness that we have the power to influence the manifestations. Our awareness and the healing of our personal and collective karma and trauma have the capacity to influence how we manifest these changes in the world. Remember, we always have choice.

For years I worked as a professional psychic medium. A good psychic knows that your fate can change on a dime if you change the inner landscape of your awareness and consciousness. Nothing is doomed or fated. An experienced psychic will lay out possibilities and potentials for you.

This is my intention for you: as you read this next section, read it with the awareness of possibilities and potentials. You decide how you want to consciously steer the unfolding of the next phase of humanity.

Remember, too, that we are looking at mechanical changes in the chart, through the lens of our current perspective and stage of evolution. We might not really be able to fully grasp the potential of these changes yet.

Most importantly, my intention for you is that this information fills you with hope and leaves you deeply inspired to continue to do the work necessary to keep evolving a world that is equitable, just, sustainable, and abundant for all.

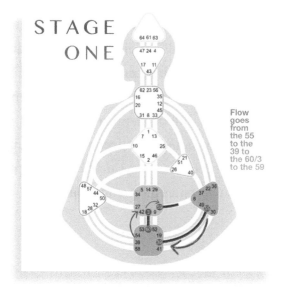

STAGE ONE

In stage one, the flow of the energy from Gate 55, the Gate of Faith, reverses and flows through Gate 39, the Gate of Re-Calibration, through Channel 60/3, the Channel of Innovation, to Gate 59, the Gate of Sustainability.

This shift in our hard wiring deepens the changes we've been exploring in how we've been creating over the last hundred years. With this shift in the charts, we move beyond the idea that our thoughts create our reality. We will be more carefully calibrated so that our faith creates our reality.

This gives us a new ability to use the power of our faith and emotional alignment, to innovate in ways that expand our sustainability and create sustainable resources. This shift also deepens our desire to share what we have with others and to create for the sake of not only sustaining yourself, but also being able to share with others.

Gate 59 is also intimately connected with the energy for reproduction and this shift in energy makes sex and sexuality more conscious and rooted in a deep spiritual connection. Creating children becomes a more deliberate and conscious act. Parenting also becomes more conscious.

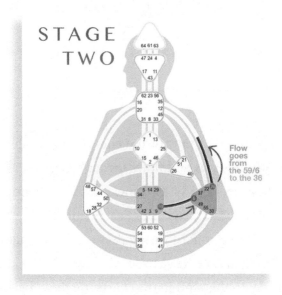

STAGE TWO

In stage two the flow of energy between Channel 59/6, the Channel of Provision, and Gate 36, the Gate of Exploration, changes. This shift in the chart changes the nature of how we experience desire and wanting. This marks the end of the energy of chaos as the pattern-interrupt that creates new human experiences.

This particular shift is a difficult one for us to imagine. We are deeply entrained to create something new from chaos. Desire drives our creative essence. We learn what we want from our experience of what we don't want.

This ends contrast as our creative driver. We now create from curiosity and the exploration of what else is possible instead of in response to an experience that is painful or unpleasant.

This shift in desire has the power to make our sexual connections more deliberate and less passionate. That doesn't mean that our sexual connections will be less satisfying, but that we have the potential to enter into our sexual relationships with more awareness and deliberation.

Passion can have a dark side. In our current experience of the waves of the Emotional Solar Plexus, we have the potential to react from the depths of the emotional wave. Not waiting out the wave creates impulsive and potentially dangerous responses that include unconscious sexual connections, fighting, and war.

With an expanded ability to consciously harness the creative capacity of emotional energy, we now have the ability to not only create more conscious intimate connections, but also the ability to create conscious and sustainable peaceful agreements. This gives us a much greater ability to create peace in the world.

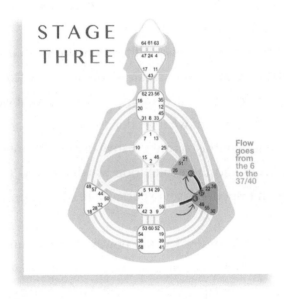

STAGE THREE

Stage three further shifts the nature of our ability to craft sustainable and peaceful agreements. With this shift, Gate 6, the Gate of Impact, flows through Channel 37/40, the Channel of Administration. This increases our ability to make peace-based long-term agreements that are rooted in our ability to create and distribute resources in a sustainable way.

The heart and the Magnetic Monopole are now calibrated by faith, emotional alignment, sustainability, equitably, and peace. Our deliberate harnessing of these energies creates a peaceful world for all, and we are able to attract and create resources for all.

We are able to make agreements that feel right and are not rooted in the "quid pro quo" of the material era. We give and share with each other because it's the right thing to do.

We consciously use our energy and our resources to lift others up because we are all well when we are all well. We are all well-fed when we are all well-fed. We are all at peace when we are all at peace.

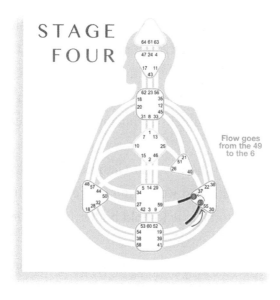

STAGE FOUR

In this final stage, the energy flow in Channel 19/49, the Channel of Intimacy and Connection, comes apart, creating the final delineation of humankind out of the animal kingdom. Gate 49, the Gate of the Catalyst, flows to Gate 6, the Gate of Impact. We are able to revolutionize the way in which we create resources, to be able to change and respond to what's needed to sustain peace and agreements.

This powerful change in the chart changes the nature of our personal, intimate bonds. Marriage and intimacy are liberated from the old limits of marriage being a tribal contract. We gain greater freedom to choose who and how we love. The nature of gender becomes more fluid. We have more choice over our intimate experiences and partnerships.

This also dramatically changes our relationship with food. Gate 19, the Gate of Attunement, is the gate that connects us to the Mammalian Circuitry. We needed to eat meat to stay grounded and connected to the energy of earth. With this break in the channel, we no longer need meat to be grounded.

This change in how we eat changes our economy and improves the health and well-being of the planet. It also allows our bodies to be able to hold higher frequencies of energy.

Our relationship with nature changes and becomes an intimate way for us to connect with Source. We are more honoring and caring with ourselves ensuring that the way in which we use the resources of the planet are more enduring and sustainable.

CONCLUSION

These changes in the energy flow in the chart changes the energetic hardwiring of the circuitry in the chart.

Gate 63, the Gate of Curiosity, now flows to the Experiential Circuit. Logic as we know it changes. Fear, the driver of logic, loses much of its hold. We learn to trust our intuitive knowingness and ourselves more.

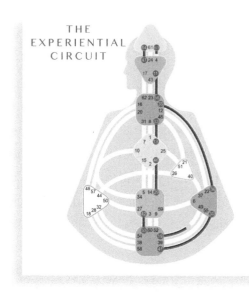

THE
EXPERIENTIAL
CIRCUIT

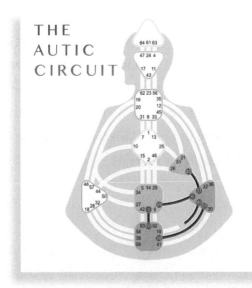

The Autic Circuit sets the stage for a profound shift from creating out of a fear of lack to creating for the sake of sustaining our abundance. This also gives us the ability to forge new, more conscious, deliberate, and intimate connections with each other.

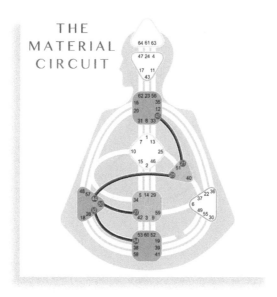

THE
MATERIAL
CIRCUIT

The "business" side of the Ego Circuit has Channel 50/27, the Channel of Sustenance, added to it. This gives us the potential for building an economy rooted in love and integrity that is driven by a desire to feed people and to amplify the quality of well-being for all.

Business becomes a vehicle for nurturing the world and profit is now measured by how much well-being your business creates.

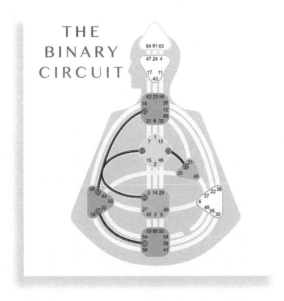

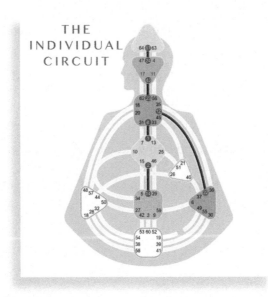

Individuality always brings with it the potential for mutation and transformation. People who carry this energy are here to be different, which has had, in the past, the potential for deep pain and suffering.

With the changes in the chart, we learn to embrace and accept authenticity and individuality. We are learning how to be different and authentic and simultaneously co-create in a common direction.

I believe that this will be the greatest adventure that we will explore as a species in the next few hundred years. How can we learn to live together with common goals and still honor who we are individually?

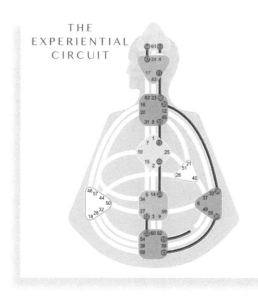

THE
EXPERIENTIAL
CIRCUIT

Gate 63, the Gate of Curiosity, now flows into Gate 64, the Gate of Divine Transference. Both of these energies are vital creative energies that use the power of asking questions as way of connecting to the Quantum Field. Prayer as a way of asking enhances our creative power. We release the need to figure out things and instead let the answers show up through our engagement with the physical world.

We connect with the natural world and our fantasy and creativity enhance what we are curious to experience. We are no longer in a need-based relationship with nature and we can merely use the beauty and awe of the physical world to enhance our connection to Source and our creative musings.

Your lesson for this chapter can be found here:

CHAPTER 7

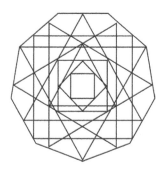

Putting It All Together

The challenge of creativity is finding the words to translate divine inspiration into manifestation. This is the first step in creating. As we've seen, words and their meanings have the power to create a photon storm in your brain, triggering a neurotransmitter response that creates emotional frequencies of energy. These energies, in turn, calibrate your essence to focus and attract your unique experience of the world.

Our conditioning influences how we interpret information, including the information about the changes in the Human Design chart. As you read this chapter, I invite you to experience how this information feels to you. If it feels right and aligned, then accept it as your truth. If it doesn't feel right and aligned, then it's not for you. I invite you to draw your own conclusions about where you think we are headed.

Be aware, as you read this information, whether your own conditioning is clouding your ability to interpret this information. I encourage you to start with a personal inventory of your de-conditioning.

The Human Design chart shows us that resiliency, the end goal of de-conditioning, is comprised of nine key traits. These key traits give you a way to assess your level of conditioning and de-conditioning.

Lovability: How much love you believe you can receive, experience, and give.

Authenticity: How free you feel to fully express your authentic self.

Courage: How well you are able to navigate through fear without letting it paralyze you.

Emotional Wisdom: Your ability to use emotional energy as a creative source of power and to be deliberate, not reactive.

Decisiveness: Your ability to know how to make decisions that are good and right for you.

Self-Trust: The degree to which you trust your inner wisdom and trust in your own abilities.

Self-Worth: Your self-esteem and your sense of your own value.

Vitality: How much energy you have to do the things you want and need to do in your life.

Empowerment: How much control and power you feel like you have over creating your life.

The more we work on living the high expression of these energies, the more control and choice we have over how we work with the changes at hand. Awakened, resilient people always have choice. People who are living out the script of their conditioning have no choice but to react with old patterns and relive the same story again and again.

So much of our personal and collective conditioning is experienced as trauma. I define trauma as any event, circumstance, or perception that causes you to lose connection with your lovability, your sense of value, and your right place in the world.

When we are traumatized, we create protective identities that are programmed to react, or we compartmentalize emotions when we encounter situations that trigger our trauma. Protective identities decrease our resiliency.

The evolution of the world is dependent on our healing of our trauma. We must reclaim our lovability, our self-worth, and find our right place in the world. The first step in doing this is rewriting the words we use in the stories we tell about who we are.

Science shows us that DNA responds to the cadence of language. We can splice DNA using radio frequency waves programmed with the cadence of language. We can even heal ancestral memories stored in the genes when we change the way we talk about ourselves.

Optimists live longer and are healthier. They use high frequency language that programs them to look for positive outcomes and improves the quality of their lives.

Words, in essence, create the world. This is the power of the Throat Center and why the Throat Center is the center that regulates action. We don't know what to create if we don't have the words first.

Words must be used with a sense of deep responsibility and obligation. The words we speak not only have the power to change our own lives, they have the power to change the lives of others. We will, through the use of our language, influence and usher in this powerful new chapter in the story of humanity.

As we travel through this transition in global cycles and the advent of the manifestation of a new human creative potential on the planet, we will, inevitably go through a cycle of disruption. Disruption is a crucial part of the evolutionary process.

We will see the fall of old collective structures and systems that are rooted in the formulaic thinking of material consciousness. Humanity will no longer allow itself to be measured by numbers. Whatever new ways of organizing ourselves we create will take into account the inherent and unique value that each of us brings into the world.

These disruptive cycles can feel frightening and destabilizing. We will lose our old identity and question who we are individually and collectively. Disruptive cycles kick us out into the unknown and force us to have to embrace a temporary state of uncertainty.

I call this state of uncertainty "the void." The void is an essential part of any cycle of rebirth and renewal. Experiencing the void is a key part of the transformational process and we all go through void cycles in our lives as part of growth.

The void can be a result of a cataclysmic or traumatic event. It can be due to astrological cycles, such as a Saturn cycle. The void is triggered by a call for change from your soul. It is your soul's way of calling you forward into a more expanded story of who you are.

The purpose of the void is to shatter your old identity. It helps you create space to redefine yourself so that you can begin to craft a new life that is more in alignment with your authentic self.

The void can feel very, very uncomfortable. This discomfort can often cause us to feel as though we want to go back to normal—to return to how things used to be. This longing makes us vulnerable to forgetting that we are moving forward. Instead of embracing the void we fight and resist it. The resistance to the change at hand is exhausting, depleting, and slows down the process of transformation.

In collective void cycles, there are always groups of people who resist the cycle of change. This creates tension and even fighting. We need people to resist the void. Conservatism is an essential part of evolution. We need people who want to hold on to the "old ways" to ensure that as we move forward and innovate, we don't throw the proverbial baby out with the bathwater. Evolution requires a certain amount of checks and balances.

The void is an important journey that helps you span the gap between who you used to be and who you want to be. The time spent in the void can be highly re-aligning, re-calibrating, and essential to cultivating the energy necessary for growth. It is a time when you are being trained to cultivate and deepen your faith.

We see, in the upcoming mutation, that learning to cultivate faith is an essential part of mastering our new quantum creative potential. We are building our faith muscle and learning to trust that we are sufficiently supported. We are healing our relationship with Source and with our higher selves so that we create from a place of "enough-ness" versus out of fear of lack.

At this stage in our evolution, we are beginning the process of entering the void, both on a personal and collective level. This is a very vulnerable time when tensions and the potential exhaustion and burnout are high. We can long to go back to the old ways—even fight to return to what was before.

There are seven key things we need to consciously cultivate to get us through the void:

1. **Support** - We need each other and a community of like-minded people to help us with this transition.

2. **Realism** - We have to be real about what we need to get through this. There is a fine line between intentionality and fantasy. Staying grounded in reality, as challenging as that can be at times, is vital. In a third-dimensional world, you still have to do things on the material plane as part of making change.

3. **Intention** - You have to make a decision about where you are headed. You will stay stuck in the discomfort of the void if you don't have a sense of where you want to go next.

4. **Faith** - You have to have the trust in Source, in your own value, and know that you are being supported, even if you don't know how the journey out of the void will unfold.

5. **Inspired Attitude** - Taking care of your mindset and keeping your focus on where you're going is vital and helps keep depletion and exhaustion at bay. Cultivating practices such as gratitude, meditation, and prayer, help you keep your energy frequency high and resilient.

6. **Creativity** - Consciously cultivating a creative practice also helps with sustaining your energy through the void cycle. Many of us have been so deeply conditioned by the seriousness of logic that we forget evolution can be fun! Reconnecting with your creative self is essential to not only helping you remember the power of fun and play, it also raises your

dopamine and serotonin levels, making it easier for you to tap into the creative flow that enhances synchronicity and serendipity helping you see the next "right step" to your journey.

7. **Sharing** - As leaders of this evolving world, the work you do on a personal level not only helps you with your own evolution and expansion. What you master becomes a key part of what you are here to share with others. Sharing keeps the heart open and helps you navigate your own path out of the void into an expanded story of who you are and what you are here to bring to the world.

The most important thing we need to get us through the void is a vision—a new story—of where we are headed. If you think about traveling on a journey, you can't get to where you're going if you don't know where you're headed.

If words create worlds and contain the frequency of energy that creates the template of what we're building, then creating a world vision that, in essence, acts a prayer field, is key to getting us from where we are now into the world of equitable, sustainable peace that we are longing for.

The mechanical changes in the Human Design chart show us the potential of the story we're in the middle of writing. This story of the evolution of humanity has been told and interpreted many different ways. If the story we tell sets the tone and the direction for what we attract and create, then we have the power to influence the direction we're headed.

We may not be able to change the mechanics of our evolution, but our stories inform us as to how we are going to get to the other side of this evolutionary void.

We can now hold the vision of a spiritual world and act to bring it through with our creative power. The stories we tell have the power to create a revolution of peace on the planet. We are warriors winning the battle over how the future of the planet will look through the power of the words we use and the corresponding actions we take.

The vision we hold cultivates the faith to trust that the innovations to feeding and sustaining the world and each other will be made, that peace is inevitable and that we will emerge from this transformative cycle a more complete and integrated expression of Spirit in form.

It is your job right now to craft a personal narrative - a new story - about the life you want to be living. I encourage you to take some time while as we enter this vital void cycle to literally write out the story of who you are, the story you want to grow into experiencing.

I also want to invite us all to write a new narrative about our world, about the way in which we want to recreate the story of humanity and elevate it to a new, more fulfilled expression of the true story of who we really are.

I leave you with my personal world vision, the one I imagine each morning in my meditation. I invite you to join me in holding this vision, or to create your own version to anchor the template of the world we are individually and collectively building.

What we create together in consciousness sets the stage for what's possible on the planet. Please join me and let's co-create using the power of our hearts and minds.

Let's imagine a world of sustainable, equitable peace - a world where everyone is abundant, well fed, and has easy access to sustainable sources of clean water.

A world where all people have easy access to integrated health care that supports the full expression of their health and vitality.

A world where all people feel loved, empowered and able to make their unique contribution to the world.

A world where we all heal the karma and the pain of the past and only bring forward the lessons and the blessings from what we've experienced and the intention to write a new story of humanity that is equitable and just.

A world where we take our direction in life from our spiritual connection and our connection to the unique, vital and irreplaceable role that only each of us can play -where we are guided by our desire to contribute to the greater good of humanity and we embrace the many diverse spiritual paths that we collectively and individually choose to follow.

Let's imagine a world where everyone is safe from war, hatred, discrimination, and terror. Where we see the heart of each other, and we honor the unique expression of each and every one of us.

A world where we are free to choose who and how we love, and we embrace the many faces and facets of love.

A world where we embody the understanding that I am because you are and without you— each and every one of you—I would not be who I am.

A world where all children are loved, nurtured, and welcomed.

Where all people are free and have easy access to education and can follow their dreams and their destinies and are celebrated on their unique journey of discovery and mastery.

Where experience is honored and valued and we understand that sometimes wisdom can only come from experience and time so that not only do we celebrate our children, we celebrate our mothers, our fathers, our grandmothers, and grandfathers.

A world where words are used to uplift, create, empower, love, and honor each other.

A world where we live in alignment with nature and where we assume our place as humble inhabitants and care for our planet and her resources with the deep awareness that each of our individual actions have the capacity to affect us all.

A world where we honor all sentient beings and serve as sacred stewards for this breath-taking and awe-inspiring planet.

We see ourselves living in a world where our natural state of wonder in connection with our true creative power is kept alive and celebrated and where everyone honors their unique gifts and knows that each life is a precious once-in-a-lifetime cosmic event.

Where the extremes of life cause us to take rapid and compassionate action for the sake of others.

Where we nurture love, value ourselves and our own unique contribution to the world.

A world where we know death is inevitable, so we dance with the vulnerability and joy of life knowing that each moment is precious and that all manifestations of life are precious.

We see a world of sustainable resources and consequently sustainable peace and we hold that vision with faith, confidence, and the open awareness that the solutions and manifestations we seek are already on their way.

And we embrace where we are right now knowing that we are exactly where we need to be, enveloped fully in the energy of Love, fully present and ready to take the next necessary steps ready to evolve the world.

Thank you for joining me in co-creating this vision. Thank you for being the unique, vital and irreplaceable part of the divine plan that you are.

I love you.

Your lesson for this chapter can be found here:

References

Amara, H. A. (2020). Inspiring people to liberate their full voice and power. Retrieved from https://heather-ashamara.com/

Baron-Reid, C. (2020). *Oracle of the 7 Energies: A 49-Card Deck and Guidebook.* Carlsbad, CA: Hay House.

Beckwith, M. B. (2019). *Prosperity, Plenitude & Infinite Possibilities.* That Guy's House.

Bernstein, G. (2018). *The Universe Has Your Back: Transform Fear to Faith.* Carlsbad, CA: Hay House.

Bernstein, G. (2019). *Super attractor: Methods for Manifesting a Life Beyond Your Wildest Dreams.* Carlsbad, CA: Hay House.

Braden, G. (2019). *The Science of Self-empowerment: Awakening the New Human Story.* Carlsbad, CA: Hay House.

Braden, G. (2020). *The Wisdom Codes: Ancient Words to Rewire Our Brains and Heal Our Hearts.* Carlsbad, CA: Hay House.

Cannon, D. (2011). *The Three Waves of Volunteers and the New Earth*. Huntsville, AR: Ozark Mountain Pub.

Chopra, D. (2019). *Metahuman: Unleashing Your Infinite Potential*. New York: Harmony Books.

Church, D. (2020). *Bliss Brain: The Neuroscience of Remodeling Your Brain for Resilience, Creativity, and Joy*. Carlsbad, CA: Hay House.

Dinan, S., & Mitchell, D. H. (2020). Shift Your World. Retrieved from https://www.theshiftnetwork.com/

Dinan, S., & Williamson, M. (2016). *Sacred America, Sacred World - Fulfilling Our Mission in Service to All*. Hampton Roads Publishing.

Dispenza, D. J. (2019). *Becoming Supernatural*. Hay House UK.

Dooley, M., & Farquhar, T. (2017). *From Deep Space With Love: A Conversation About Consciousness, the Universe, and Building a Better World*. Carlsbad, CA: Hay House.

Dooley, M., & Proctor, B. (2019). *Infinite Possibilities: The Art of Living Your Dreams*. New York: Atria Paperback.

Dooley, M. (2019). *Playing the Matrix*. Hay House UK.

Goswami, A., & Onisor, V. (2019). *Quantum Spirituality: The Pursuit of Wholeness*.

Hancock, G. (2019). *America Before: The Key to Earth's Lost Civilization*. London: Coronet, an imprint of Hodder & Stoughton.

Harris, L. (2019). *Energy Speaks: Messages From Spirit on Living, Loving, and Awakening*. New World Library.

Hicks, E., Hicks, J., & Abraham. (2011). *Getting Into the Vortex: Guided Meditations CD and User Guide.* Carlsbad, CA: Hay House.

Lee, I. F. (2020). *Joyful: The Surprising Power of Ordinary Things to Create Extraordinary Happiness.* Little Brown Spark.

Lipton, B. H. (2016). *The Biology of Belief: Unleashing the Power of Consciousness, Matter & Miracles.* Carlsbad, CA: Hay House.

McKusick, E. D. (2014). *Tuning the Human Biofield: Healing With Vibrational Sound Therapy.* Rochester, VT: Healing Arts Press.

McKusick, E. D. (2021). *Electric Body, Electric Health: Using the Electromagnetism Around and Within You to Rewire, Recharge, and Raise Your Voltage.* St. Martins Essentials.

McTaggart, L. (2018). *The Power of Eight: Harnessing the Miraculous Energies of a Small Group to Heal Others, Your Life, and the World.* Atria Books.

Myss, C. (2020). *Intimate Conversations with the Divine: Prayer, Guidance, and Grace.* Carlsbad, CA: Hay House.

Nordby, J. (2020). *The Creative Cure: How Finding and Freeing Your Inner Artist Can Heal Your Life.* Hierophant Publishing.

Nordby, J. (2016). *Blessed are the Weird: A Manifesto for Creatives.* Boise, ID: Manifesto Publishing House.

Pauley, T. (2003). *I'm Rich Beyond My Wildest Dreams: How to Get Everything You Want in Life.* Berkley.

Pauley, T. (2019). *In the Presence of the Generous One: The Miracle Healing You Created*. Rich Dreams Publishing.

Perrakis, A. (2019). *The Book of Blessings and Rituals: Magical Invocations for Healing, Setting Energy, and Creating Sacred Space*. Fair Winds Press.

Peru, E. (2018). *Cosmic Messengers: The Universal Secrets to Unlocking Your Purpose and Becoming Your Own Life Guide*. Carlsbad, CA: Hay House.

Radin, D. I. (2018). *Real Magic*. New York: Harmony.

Redfield, J. (2018). *The Celestine Prophecy*. Grand Central Publishing.

Sark, & Waddell, J. (2015). *Succulent Wild Love: Six Powerful Habits for Feeling More Love More Often*. Novato, CA: New World Library.

Sheldrake, R. (2020). *The Science Delusion*. Hodder Stoughton.

Silverman, L. K. (2002). *Upside-down Brilliance: The Visual-Spatial Learner*. Denver, CO: DeLeon Publishing.

Tolle, E. (2018). *A New Earth: Awakening to Your Life's Purpose*. UK: Penguin Books.

Tsabary, S., & Jain, R. (2020). *Superpowered: Transform Anxiety Into Courage, Confidence, and Resilience*. New York: Random House.

Williamson, M. (2019). *A Politics of Love: A Handbook for a New American Revolution*. New York: HarperOne.

Yehuda, R., Kahana, B., Southwick, S. M., & Giller, E. L. (1976, January 01). Depressive features in holocaust survivors with post-traumatic stress disorder. Retrieved December 11, 2020, from https://link.springer.com/article/10.1007/BF02103016

About the Author

Karen Curry Parker is an expert in Quantum Human Design and developed a system to help explore the relationship between Quantum Physics and Human Design. She's the creator of Quantum Conversations, a successful podcast with over 90,000 downloads in less than twelve months, and two systems of Human Design: Quantum Human Design™ and the Quantum Alignment System™. Multiple news outlets, radio shows, and tele-summits have featured her work on their programs.

Karen is also the author of numerous bestselling books all designed to help you create the life you were destined to live and find and embrace the purpose of your existence.

Karen is available for private consultations, keynote talks, and to conduct in-house seminars and workshops.

You can reach her at <u>Karen@quantumalignmentsystem.com.</u>

To run your chart with the new Quantum Human design language go to *FreeHumanDesignChart.com* & to find out more about Quantum Alignment visit *https://www.quantumalignmentsystem.com/*

Find more great books published by Human Design Press.
https://gracepointpublishing.com/human-de-
sign-press-publisher

Made in the USA
Monee, IL
03 June 2023